God's Girls!  #1

For Kenzie
on her 11th
birthday—
love, Uncle Robert
& Aunt Karon

God's Girls! #1

Karen H. Whiting

LEGACY PRESS®

Dedicated to my daughter Darlene Elizabeth Whiting and her friend Daniella Alves (my adopted daughter in Christ), who always strive to be creative and follow Jesus.

GOD'S GIRLS!/BOOK 1
©2003 by Karen H. Whiting, fifth printing
ISBN 1-58411-020-1
Legacy reorder# LP48011

Legacy Press
P.O. Box 261129
San Diego, CA 92196

Illustrator: Aline Heiser
Editor: Christy Allen

Printed in the United States of America

Contents

✳ ✳ ✳ ✳ ✳ ✳ ✳ ✳ ✳ ✳ ✳ ✳

Welcome!

This book is about **GOD**,

the **CREATOR**,

and how God **CREATIVELY** used women in the Bible,

and **YOU**, a young woman,

CREATIVELY CREATED, becoming

a more **CREATIVE** person and

more like **JESUS!**

Now let's think about the 5 W's of this book: that is, the

* who?
* what?
* where?
* when? and
* why?

WHO?

Who are these women and who are **you?**

The women in this book were ordinary women who responded to God. These women showed faith in their actions.

Their stories are told in God's Word as examples for all people, showing how God uses ordinary women to do extraordinary things.

Do you ever wonder, *Who am I and why did God make me?* You are a child of God. God loves you and has a plan for you.

Remember:

✳ **You** are becoming a woman.

✳ **You** are made in God's image.

✳ **God** created you and created plans for you.

✳ **You** are a creative person.

✳ **You have great potential!**

What can you make and what can you do with what you make?

This book gives you a start on becoming more creative. The directions for crafts help you learn to make something. You can learn to weave, sculpt, cut shapes, and other types of crafting. You will learn basic skills to build upon.

The **sparkling ideas** help you see what else you can make once you learn to craft an item, creating more crafts by using the same general directions. Let these sparks of imaginative ideas light a spark of other ideas in your mind. Think of each craft as merely a beginning.

What else?

Discover what you enjoy making and doing. These crafts let you develop your ability and talents. The book includes

Read On! ⇨

suggestions for what to do with many of the crafts. Always remember that you can make crafts as gifts for loved ones, special people and people in need.

The crafts remind you of God's Word and God's people. Each craft is linked to a woman in the Bible for a special reason — to serve as a reminder of how God used that woman. Note the virtues in these women that please God and help others. As you make the crafts, use them or give them to others and think about how God can use you, too. As you discover how easy it is to create something beautiful, think of how easy it is for God to help you develop virtues and become a woman of God.

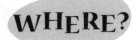

Where do you do your creating and where should you put everything — completed crafts, crafts in progress, supplies to use and craft tools?

This is a practical decision that requires advance planning. Consider these ideas before choosing your crafting place:

✱ Find a place where you have room for your supplies and room to work, a place that does not disrupt family life.

✱ Work where it's okay to make a mess as long as you will clean it up.

✱ Remember to consider the mess that might occur. If you are using paint, cover the floors and tables with plastic. An old tablecloth, shower curtain or painting drop cloth works well. If you don't have these, cut open a heavy plastic trash bag to use. Wear old clothes.

✱ If you need to clean up before you finish a project, find a box or plastic container to keep your supplies organized until you have time to finish the project.

✳ If you want a friend to make a craft with you, choose a place with enough room for two or more.

Where should you read this book and write in it? Find a comfortable, quiet place to read. Consider:

✳ A place with room for this book and your Bible in case you want to look up more about the Bible women.

✳ A place where a friend with the same book can read with you and share thoughts. Somewhere you can read, talk and laugh together.

✳ A place with a table might be good, but some girls prefer to spread out on the floor or a bed. Anywhere you are comfortable is fine.

✳ Find a special place to keep this book and your Bible when not in use, like a book case or a basket.

WHEN?

When should you make things?

Making crafts takes time, so plan to be creative when you have enough time to set up, make your project and clean up. Read the directions and consider how long it might take. Girls work at different speeds, so this book does not give time limits. It's fun to be fast, but it is also fun to be slow and enjoy the creative process. Enjoy the feel of the materials as they take shape and transform into something new.

When should you start?

Start after you gather everything needed to make the craft. Check the list of materials and supplies. Have an adult do a safety check, and make sure you are capable of using any tools safely. Have proper ventilation. Also, don't start until you finish setting up.

When should you stop and clean up? STOP

Clean up when you are done. If you can't finish in one day, stop about 10-15 minutes before you need to do something else. Clean up and cover liquids, such as paints and glues. Make the area look neat. Make a note of which step you finished and where to begin when you have time to return. Clean up any spills. Wet paint or wet glue is easier to clean than dried paint or dried glue!

Clean-up check list:

* Clean brushes with soap and water.
* Clean tools and dry them well.
* Return tools to where they belong.
* Clean the table or work area with a sponge, broom or brush.
* Clean yourself (face, hands, fingernails).
* Clean the floor around the craft area.

Why should you give things you make as a gift?

God's Word says that He loves a generous giver, so give when your heart wants to give. Give with love. Give when you see someone in need who touches your heart and you know you can make something to help ease the pain. Give when you want to show someone you love that you care about him or her, even if it isn't a birthday! Give to bring joy to another person or give as a way to open up a discussion about God and create an opportunity to tell someone what Jesus means to you.

Also feel good when keeping crafts for yourself. Each craft can help you remember God and His women.

Why make things?

◎ **Because** God made things and making things helps you know God better. As you create, you see the joy in creating. When you look at what you made, you understand how God could look at all He made and see it was good.

◎ **Because** being creative helps develop talents and skills. Some things will be easier to make than others because of skills you already know.

◎ **Because** you are made in God's image, in the image of the most creative being in the universe. Creativity is part of God and part of God's image that is in you. You may not be creative in the same way as a friend, but you are creative. There are many ways of being creative: creative in drawing,

12 Read On! ⇨

creative in social skills, creative in organizing skills or creative in thinking.

◎ **Because** becoming more creative helps you become a woman. As you watch simple materials transform into new forms, you can understand there is a process to bring about change. Likewise, there is a process in growing and changing into a woman.

◎ **Because** crafts help you discover how beauty is created from different materials. Crafts help you appreciate what is created by others and by God. God created each person to be beautiful in an individual way. As you grow and transform into a woman, let God show you the special beauty within yourself.

As you read about each woman in this book, you will find a quality of beauty God saw — a virtue connected with the craft that will remind you of your ability to develop the same trait.

Creating things helps develop virtues!

✳ Take time to create and develop patience.

✳ Make something to give and develop generosity.

✳ Follow directions and develop obedience.

✳ Take pleasure in your creations and develop joy.

✳ Respond to needs by making gifts and develop a loving heart.

✳ Learn to set up and clean up and develop responsibility.

Supplies

Let's look at the supplies and tools you will need for most of the crafts:

Scissors and cutting tools   There are many types of scissors, from tiny manicure scissors to large kitchen shears. Other cutting tools include craft knives, mat knives and cutting wheels (see more about these on the next page). Match the correct cutting tool to each project.

Fabric scissors   These need to be sharp. Cutting paper and cardboard with fabric scissors quickly dulls the blades, so ask someone which scissors in the house are set aside as fabric scissors.

Craft scissors   Usually a heavier-duty scissors than fabric scissors, this type cuts craft foam, light cardboard and paper.

Small craft scissors   School scissors and other small scissors are good for cutting paper, especially if you have to get into small places and cut lots of curves.

Cutting wheel   Sold in sewing and craft stores, this is a tool with a rotating wheel at the end of a handle. The wheel can be changed. Wheels can cut straight edges, or if you use a fancy wheel with a rippled or scalloped-type edge, it will cut a fancy edge. The wheel can cut a few layers of fabric at one time. Try it on sample fabric first to learn how fast it cuts, and how to follow curves and straight lines.

Craft knife   Get an adult to help you use a craft knife. This is a metal tool with a very sharp blade. Stores sell small, disposable craft knives as well as long-lasting tools

Read On!⇨

with replaceable blades. These cut through heavy cardboard, mat board and other medium-weight materials. However, you must be careful not to cut yourself. As with any knife, a craft knife is sharp and can easily cut skin. Always place a cutting board under the material you are cutting so you won't cut or scratch the table. Be careful to hold your fingers away from the blade where they won't get cut. Don't pull the knife toward your body, but push the knife away from your body.

Mat knife Similar to a craft knife but larger and uses a razor blade as the cutting blade.

Saw Saws can easily cut skin and bones so ask an adult to cut for you or train you and watch when you use one. These are workshop tools and should only be used by someone who has been trained to use them. Some are hand saws and some are power tools.

Glue and Adhesive

There are many types of glue in stores. It can be difficult to know which one to use (see below)! Each material requires a certain type of glue for it to bond and hold together. Read the labels of glue containers to learn more about how each one works. Read labels carefully to check for safety, too.

Foam glue Glues with petroleum will melt foam, or eat it away. This clear glue has no petroleum in it. It also glues craft foam.

Craft glue This is the white glue often used in schools. It bonds paper or cardboard but does not hold fabric or heavier materials together.

Paste Paste is made from flour. When it dries it often crumbles and falls apart. It is only a temporary glue and not useful for crafts.

Tacky glue This is a thick, white glue that dries clear. It bonds many materials together (but not foam). It costs more, but your crafts will last longer.

Spray adhesive These usually contain petroleum. Often, both surfaces must be sprayed to be glued. The spray adhesive may bleed through paper and thin materials, so test it first on a scrap. Sprays have fumes, so they need to be used in a well-ventilated room (one with good air flow and with a vent or open window that allows the fumes to escape).

Hot glue gun This glue gets hot and can burn your skin, so ask an adult to help you. The glue comes in a stick and must be used in a special gun that is heated with electricity. Always keep a container of water nearby to cool your skin in case of a burn. The glue cools quickly and bonds many materials. Try it on scrap materials first to see if the glue will hold. Place your glue gun on a protective pad (heavy cardboard covered with foil, or an old computer mouse pad) when you are not using it.

Safety

Always be careful when making crafts. Spills, sharp tools and hot glue can be dangerous. Look and think before you do things so that you avoid mistakes and work safely. If small children are nearby, remember that they can choke on tiny objects or cut themselves if tools are in their reach.

Joyful Crafts

Like fireworks in the **heart**,

Joy explodes with colors,

Crackles with **excitement**

and **energizes** the soul.

Let joy fill your heart as you grow closer to God. As you become a woman, you are growing and changing — in mind, body and soul. In this section, discover women who exploded with joy as they developed their souls (the spiritual part of themselves). Learn how these joyful women followed God's commands. Enjoy making tools and artful reminders about prayer, journaling, praise and God's joyous love.

God's Love Fills Me With Joy

Memory Verse

Then Miriam the prophetess, Aaron's sister, took a tambourine in her hand, and all the women followed her, with tambourines and dancing. –Exodus 15:20

Miriam

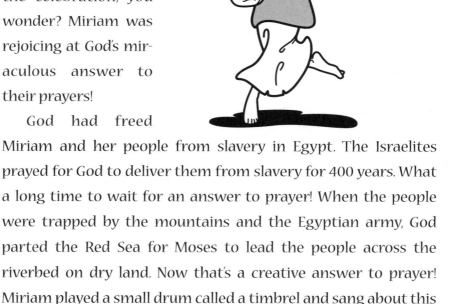

Miriam, Moses' and Aaron's sister, sang and led a parade. Why all the celebration, you wonder? Miriam was rejoicing at God's miraculous answer to their prayers!

God had freed Miriam and her people from slavery in Egypt. The Israelites prayed for God to deliver them from slavery for 400 years. What a long time to wait for an answer to prayer! When the people were trapped by the mountains and the Egyptian army, God parted the Red Sea for Moses to lead the people across the riverbed on dry land. Now that's a creative answer to prayer! Miriam played a small drum called a timbrel and sang about this victory from God.

Do you ever feel like Miriam — so happy that you want to cheer and shout with joy? In Psalm 23, the psalmist was so thankful for what God supplied that he wrote, "My cup overflows."

It's fun to celebrate answers to prayer, but it's also easy to forget or overlook them. To help you remember how God answers your prayers, weave the Cup of Blessings. Fill the cup with your answers to prayer. Weave in jingle bells to shake the cup with joy!

Prayer

Dear Lord, thank You for filling my days with love. Help me to see Your answers in life and rejoice in Your love. Amen.

Dazzling Thoughts

- ◎ In this craft, yarn and a broken cup make something beautiful. God uses what seems broken in people's lives and weaves it together for good — for something spiritually beautiful. Look up this Scripture in your Bible: Romans 8:28.

- ◎ When you feel down, pull prayer answers from your cup and remember all that God has done for you. When you add a new prayer answer to the cup, give it a celebration shake!

- ◎ Proverbs 31:19 says, "In her hand she holds the distaff and grasps the spindle with her fingers." A distaff is the staff on which the wool or other fiber is wound for spinning into yarn. The spindle is the rod used in spinning the thread.

- ◎ Yarn comes in plys, a number of strands that are twisted together. The more strands, the stronger the yarn. Christians can also "twist together" by working in unity. The more we join together for God's work, the greater our strength, too!

19

 # Journaling

Sometimes a problem turns into a blessing. I remember one

when : _____

_____

_____

_____

_____

My best prayer answers were: _____

_____

_____

_____

_____

_____

Right now, my biggest prayer request is: _____

_____

_____

_____

Maybe God sees the answer differently. How else might God

answer my prayer? _____

_____

_____

_____

_____

Cool Craft * Cup of Blessings

What You'll Need:

* plastic cup
* yarn
* jingle bells
* scissors or craft knife

What To Do:

1. Draw an odd number of lines from the top of the cup to the bottom, evenly-spaced, around the cup. (You can use any size of cup but larger cups are easier to work with.)

2. Cut the lines with scissors or a craft knife, stopping ¼" above the bottom of the cup. These strips are called "spokes."

3. Tie the end of the yarn around the bottom of one spoke. Turn

the knot so that it is on the inside of the cup.

4. Weave the yarn behind one spoke, then in front of the next spoke. Continue alternating the yarn in front and behind each spoke all the way around and up the cup. Continue going around until you are 1" below the top of the cup.

5. Just before you reach the top of the cup, string jingle bells onto the yarn. Slide the bell in front of that spoke (outside of cup). Every other spoke should have a jingle bell.

6. To end the yarn, pull it back on the inside of the cup around a final spoke. Knot and then cut it, leaving about 3" of yarn. Push the end of the yarn down inside the yarn of one spoke on the inside of the cup.

✳ Sparkling Ideas ✳

◎ Try cutting slits that are not evenly spaced — even curving slits. This will create a curvy pattern in the weaving.

◎ Use two colors of yarn at once. (This is harder!) Weave one color of yarn in front of a spoke. Then weave the second color behind the same spoke. Cross the two colors, then cover the next spoke. You will get a striped pattern!

◎ Try changing colors to weave pictures!

◎ Make a cup with white yarn. Then with fabric markers, color a design on the cup.

✳ ✳ ✳ ✳ ✳ ✳ ✳ ✳ ✳

God's Love Fills My Mind with Wisdom

Memory Verse

Blessed is she who has believed that what the Lord has said to her will be accomplished!
–Luke 1:45

Elizabeth

Two pregnant women greeted each other. Elizabeth used strange words of greeting. Instead of just telling her cousin Mary that she was glad to see her, she said Mary was "blessed." "Blessed" means to be in God 's favor. When a baby grows inside the womb, the mother feels the baby kick and move inside her. When Mary came to visit Elizabeth, Elizabeth's baby jumped with joy inside her.

God caused Elizabeth's baby to jump as a sign to her that Mary was blessed — she was pregnant with His Son. Elizabeth was righteous and obedient to God's commandments. This story is a reminder that people who believe God's Word will be blessed.

Elizabeth's baby was also a miracle. She had always wanted a baby but at an old age she and her husband still did not have children. God answered her prayer with her son, John the

Baptist. You can read about Elizabeth in Luke 1:5-45.

Believers are blessed with wisdom and fruits of the Spirit. This craft will show you how to decorate a basket with fruit. Use the basket to hold a journal. Write in your journal what God's Word means to you. Record the blessings in your life!

Prayer

God, help me to understand Your words and hold them in my heart. Amen.

Dazzling Thoughts

◎ In the Bible, baskets provided a means of escape from enemies (Exodus 2:3). Moses was placed in a basket as an infant to protect his life. The disciples rescued Paul — then called "Saul" from enemies in a basket (Acts 9:23-25).

◎ This journaling basket will help keep you close to God because you will be reading and reflecting on His Word. This is a good protection from temptations!

◎ "Fruits" in the Bible also refer to the fruits of the Holy Spirit. Fruits such as love, joy and peace are produced in the Christian life when we let the Spirit enlighten us and guide us. Read about the fruits of the Spirit in Galatians 5:22-23.

 Journaling

Baskets remind me of : _____

_____

_____

_____

_____

I was once a baby inside my mother, too. I wonder what I did in

there. God saw me, and formed me then. I think: _____

_____

_____

_____

_____

_____

I want to be blessed. Today I can show I believe God's Word by:

_____

_____

_____

I'm going to keep my journaling basket _____

_____

and I will try to journal _____

_____

_____

Cool Craft! Fruitful Journaling Basket

What You'll Need:

* basket with handle
* tiny plastic fruit
* florist wire (if needed)
* craft scissors
* foam glue
* straight pin

What To Do:

1. Fruit with wire attached to it will work best for this craft. You can find this at a craft store, usually in the artificial flower section. If you do not have this type, you can attach the wire to the fruit by winding it around the stem and leaving long ends of wire. If the fruit does not have a stem, use a pin to make an opening, roll the tip of the wire into glue and then push the wire into the fruit (see diagram). Let it dry overnight before you continue this craft.

2. You can leave wired fruit grouped or separate it into individual pieces, each on a wire.

3. Arrange the fruit around the basket handle so you can figure out how you think it looks best.

4. Twist the wire around the handle and fasten the fruit in place.

5. Place a Bible, pen and notebook (for journaling!) inside the basket.

Sparkling Ideas

◎ Sparkle the fruit with clear glitter! Before attaching the fruit to your basket, roll it in glue and then roll it in glitter. Let it dry before you attach it to the basket.

◎ Paint the basket (but check with an adult first!). Spray the basket a solid color. To be a less messy painter, put the basket in a box to spray it. Always use spray paint outside or in a room with an open window.

◎ Sponge paint the basket. Use a sponge and fabric or acrylic paints to paint designs on it. An eraser tip works well for painting grapes or blueberries. Remember that just like a sponge soaks up liquid, you want to soak in God's Word!

◎ Use a permanent marker to write the names of the fruits of the Spirit on the basket.

◎ Tie a pretty bow onto the basket. God's Word and how we act because of it binds (or ties) us together with Him.

God's Love Gives Me Strength

Memory Verse

And now, my daughter, don't be afraid. I will do for you all you ask. All my fellow townsmen know that you are a woman of noble character. –Ruth 3:11

Ruth

How does a woman come from poverty and the death of her husband to become a shining star? Ruth shows us how.

After her husband died, Ruth left her town with Naomi, her mother-in-law, and went to Naomi's town to take care of her. Naomi's husband had died, too, so she was alone. Ruth did not complain in the new town. Instead, she asked Naomi if she should work on a farm picking up leftover food. Ruth followed Naomi's advice on where to gather — or "glean" — the food.

God gave the people laws about gleaning. Gleaning allowed the poor to work for food. Ruth shared what she picked. She ate only what she needed and gave the rest to Naomi.

God blessed Ruth greatly. Boaz, the owner of the farm where she gleaned, married Ruth. One of Ruth's grandchildren, David, later became an important king. Ruth and David were also special for another reason: they were ancestors of Jesus.

Ruth let God be the center of her life and trusted Him to help her. Make this candle holder as a reminder to put God's Word in the center of your life.

Prayer

God, thank You for giving me the Bible, Your Word, as a light unto my path. Help me remember that like Ruth, I can succeed with Your help. Amen.

Dazzling Thoughts

◎ The Bible talks about light in many ways. God's Word is called a "lamp" and a "light" (Psalm 119:105). Jesus declared, "I am the light of the world" (John 8:12). The Bible tells us to be lights (Matthew 5:14). Light comes in many forms!

◎ Candlelight can be used to light other candles.

◎ You can transform a can into a pretty candle holder, just as God transforms you so people will see your beauty and excellence.

◎ A gentle breeze or even a person's breath can blow out a candle, but the candle can be relit. When you feel discouraged, turn again to God and allow Him to relight your heart with joy and enlighten you with His Word.

Journaling

Today I read my Bible. I want to do what God says. What I read

reminds me to : _____

_____

_____

_____

A candle glows while the wax melts. God's love can melt away

problems. My biggest problem right now is: _____

_____

_____

_____

_____

Ruth worked hard. I am willing to work hard at: _____

_____

_____

God's Word can give me bright new ideas. Today I discovered:

_____

_____

_____

Cool Craft! I Can Candle

What You'll Need:

* empty tuna or cat food cans
* gift wrap or cotton fabric scraps
* star stickers
* clay or florist's foam block
* artificial flowers
* pen
* paper
* toothpick
* long, tapered candle
* scissors
* craft glue

What To Do:

1. Clean out the can and allow it to dry.

2. Wrap the fabric or gift wrap around the can. Cut it so that it is about ½" taller than the can.

3. Glue the covering to the can with the ½" above the can top.

4. Turn the ½" edge down and glue it inside the can.

5. Decorate the fabric with star stickers.

6. Fill the can with foam or clay. If you use foam, use a craft knife to cut it so that it will fit.

7. Make a hole for the candle in the clay or foam. Place the candle in the hole. Add more clay or bits of foam until the candle stands straight.

8. Write "Philippians 4:13" on a small rectangle of paper. Glue the paper to the top of a toothpick. Stick the toothpick in the clay or foam.

9. Decorate around the candle by sticking flowers in the foam or clay.

Sparkling Ideas

◎ Add gold or silver trim to the upper edge of the can.

◎ Use the candle as a dinner centerpiece. Let each person tell what they want to do someday, no matter how impossible it seems. Discuss how these dreams can happen. Then pray, remembering that we can do all things through Christ.

◎ For a different filling in the can, use dirt and plant marigold or other tiny flower seeds in the dirt. It takes time for seeds to grow. Change takes time, too. Ruth did not become a new wife, mother or grandmother in one day!

◎ When you feel down, light the candle (but remember to get adult permission first and practice fire safety rules). Watch the candle glow and give off light. Pray for God to give you a joyful thought.

God's Love Saves Me

Memory Verse

Coming up to them at that very moment, she gave thanks to God and spoke about the child to all who were looking forward to the redemption of Jerusalem. –Luke 2:38

Anna

Anna was a member of a large family, a tribe of Israel. She married, but her husband died just seven years later. Anna lived at the temple in Jerusalem for the rest of her life. In the temple, Anna served God by worshiping, praying and fasting. She filled her days with thoughts of Him.

Anna waited a long time for the Savior. When Mary and Joseph brought baby Jesus to the temple, Anna recognized Him as the Savior. How wonderful to see and recognize the Savior! She praised God and told everyone of the wonders of God, who had finally sent a redeemer, a Savior!

Anna allowed herself to be Jesus' greatest fan at that time, even though He was just a baby. His parents held and carried Him into the temple. How did Anna know He was the Savior? She learned by being close to God. God reveals truth to believers — to His fans — to those who worship Him.

Make this fan and fill it with words of praise. When you open it, remember to keep your heart and mind open to God.

Prayer

Thank You, God, for sending Jesus. You made each person and all You made is good. Lord, help me see the good in all people. Amen.

Dazzling Thoughts

◎ A fan moves air and cools people. As a fan of Jesus, you can help move hearts. Read 2 Timothy 1:6. It talks about fanning into a flame the gift of God.

◎ This fan is made up of three hearts. There are also three persons in the trinity: God the Father, God the Son and the Holy Spirit. They are united in one. Think of one reason to praise each personality of God.

◎ God is great. It is not that God needs praise, but we need to give praise. When we praise God, we think of Him instead of thinking of ourselves or our problems. When we praise God we also remember how a great God can do mighty things. This helps us trust in God.

Journaling

God is fantastic! I know He did many things like : _____

_____

_____

_____

_____

I think Anna recognized Jesus as the Savior because: _____

_____

_____

_____

_____

Some people saw baby Jesus as just a baby. Anna saw what He

would become and what He would do. God sees what I will

become. I'd like to become: _____

_____

_____

Cool Craft! Fan-Tas-Tick

What You'll Need:

* heavy poster board
* markers
* stickers (optional)
* scissors
* hole punch

God the Son
Praise Jesus, Lord and Savior, giving eternal life

God the Father
Praise God for all He has made

God the Holy Spirit
Praise God for giving us

What To Do:

1. Cut three of the same size of paper heart from poster board. Cut slits into the hearts as shown at right.

2. Punch a hole in the bottom point of each heart. Make the hole in the same place on all three hearts.

3. Decorate the hearts with markers and stickers.

4. Slide a paper fastener through the holes to join the hearts together.

5. Slide the slits together to join the hearts.

❋ ❋ ❋ ❋ ❋ ❋ ❋ ❋ ❋

36

Sparkling Ideas

◎ On each heart of the fan write the name of one person of the Trinity. Next to the name, write a praise.

◎ Tie little ribbons or pieces of yarn around the paper fastener.

◎ Use a wooden craft stick to make a handle. Have someone help you drill a hole in the end of the stick. Then put the paper fastener through the hole. After all, God promises to "stick" with you always! Read that in Matthew 28:20.

◎ Make the fan out of plastic lids from drink containers so it is more durable.

◎ Make fans for neighbors. Write the name of your church, service times and address. Pass them out as invitations to attend!

God's Love Opens My Heart

Memory Verse

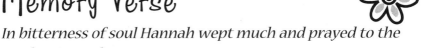

In bitterness of soul Hannah wept much and prayed to the Lord. –1 Samuel 1:10

Hannah

Hannah cried as she prayed. She opened up her deepest feelings to God, who listened and answered Hannah's prayer. What did she want so much? Like Elizabeth, she prayed for a baby. The next year, she gave birth to a son!

Hannah's request and answer are parts of prayer. Prayer is a conversation. Hannah poured out her heart to God and He answered by giving her a son. But Hannah needed to say more than, "Please give me a son." Hannah joyfully thanked God for her child, Samuel, after he was born.

Hannah made a promise to God when she prayed. She told God that if He gave her a son, she would dedicate him to God and bring him to serve in the temple. Hannah remembered her promise. So when he was old enough, Samuel went with Hannah to work in the temple. He became a great leader for God. God was pleased with Hannah and gave her five more children.

Make this heart prayer chain as a reminder to pray from the heart and to keep talking with God.

Prayer

God, thank You for being with me and always listening. Help me to remember to say "thank You" and to talk with You from my heart. Amen.

Dazzling Thoughts

◎ The paper hearts in the prayer chain are open. Prayer from the heart needs to come from an open heart that is listening for God's response.

◎ The paper prayer chain is linked together. One heart enfolds another. Prayer links a person with God. It enfolds the person praying in God's love.

◎ When a link breaks, the whole chain is broken. When you stop praying, it breaks the communication line with God. But you can always re-link because God is always ready to listen.

◎ "Devote yourselves to prayer, being watchful and thankful." Colossians 4:2

 # Journaling

When I'm happy and excited I want to tell others. God, You

want to hear that, too. What makes me happy is : _____

_____

_____

_____

_____

One of the feelings in my heart right now is: _____

_____

_____

_____

_____

Hannah prayed year after year for a son. Eventually, God gave

her a son. One thing I keep praying about is: _____

_____

_____

God answers me in His Word. Today I read: _____

_____

_____

God's Word tells me: _____

_____

_____

_____

Cool Craft! Heart Prayer Chains

What You'll Need:

* white paper
* construction paper
* star stickers
* pen
* scissors

What To Do:

1. Trace the pattern on the next page on a piece of white paper and cut it out.

2. Fold a sheet of construction paper twice. Place the pattern on the folds as indicated and trace it.

3. Cut out the inside of the heart, then cut out the outside. Unfold the heart. Make as many as you want!

41

4. Link the hearts together, sliding one heart inside the opening of another heart until it "locks" at the bottom.

5. Write a prayer request or a prayer on each heart. Add hearts as you add prayer requests and prayers.

6. When God answers a prayer request, decorate the heart with a star sticker. On the heart, write how God answered the prayer.

7. You could also write Scriptures on the hearts, or other things you hear about God and how He answers prayer. After all, God also uses people to share His Word!

8. Watch the chain grow longer and see how you and God talk through prayer.

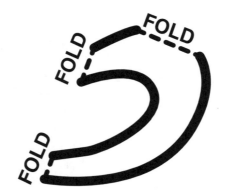

Sparkling Ideas

◎ Make a prayer chain as a family prayer activity.

◎ Use a long prayer chain at Christmas as a garland around the tree. It will be like wrapping the tree in love.

◎ When you feel sad, read the starred hearts and rejoice in God's answers.

◎ Hang a prayer chain across a wall in your room to decorate the wall with love letters between you and God! Read 2 Corinthians 3:3 that speaks of people as letters written on tablets of the heart.

◎ When you are done with a prayer chain, see if there are special answers you want to remember. Save the starred hearts with the answers in an album.

God's Love Fills Me With Laughter

Memory Verse

Sarah said, "God has brought me laughter, and everyone who hears about this will laugh with me." –Genesis 21:6

Sarah

Angels heard Sarah laugh. Sarah's laughter was the first recorded laughing in the Bible. What caused Sarah's laughter? She had eavesdropped on angels and thought their words must be a joke! What did they say?

The angels told her husband Abraham, who was already 99 years old, that Sarah and he would have a baby. The idea of having a baby in her old age made Sarah laugh. But God was not joking. Sarah gave birth to a son within a year. When Sarah looked at her baby, she felt pleasure — enough to name him Isaac, which means "laughter." She told others how God brought her laughter.

God likes to bring people joy and make them laugh. Sarah shared her joy in the Lord with others. We need to let others know that God gives us joy. Think of what brings you laughter and joy. Think of answers to prayer that made you feel happy.

Then tell someone else about it. Put the mementos of these thoughts in a container — a Joy Box!

Prayer

Lord, fill me with laughter. Let me rejoice when I look at the beauty You made. Amen.

Dazzling Thoughts

◎ Recycling a shoe box, like you will do when you make the Joy Box, helps save natural resources. In the same way, recycling happy thoughts saves tears.

◎ When you feel sad or upset, take out your Joy Box and think about what's in it. That will brighten your day! Read Philippians 4:6-8 to discover what the Bible tells us to do when we feel anxious.

◎ Read John 15:11 to find out what Jesus said about joy.

 Journaling

My favorite joke is: _____

_____

_____

_____

_____

The person who makes me laugh the most is: _____

_____

_____

Proverbs 17:22 states, "A cheerful heart is good medicine." I think

this is because: _____

_____

_____

_____

_____

Some people think of the letters of JOY as an abbreviation for

Jesus-Others-Yourself. This is a reminder that to have real joy we need to think in that order. Put Jesus first and yourself last.

Today, to put Jesus first, I will: _____

_____

_____

To put others before myself, I will: _____

_____

_____

Cool Craft! Joy Box

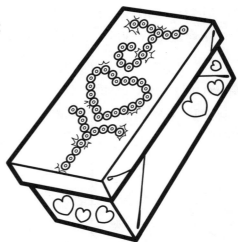

What You'll Need:

* shoe box
* gift wrap
* stickers
* markers
* scissors
* glue
* clear tape

What To Do:

1. Cover the box with gift wrap. Cover the lid separately. Use glue or tape to secure the paper.

2. Write JOY and the memory verse on the lid. Or write the memory verse on a paper heart and glue it on the lid.

3. Decorate the box with stickers and drawings.

4. Fill the box with items that make you smile, such as photos of friends, cartoons and even cards that you have received.

Sparkling Ideas

◎ Use a wooden box with a lid for a more permanent Joy Box. Paint the box, then add stickers and designs.

◎ Use a plastic shoe box or cosmetics box. You will not need to cover it with paper, but you can decorate it. Write on the plastic with permanent markers.

◎ Cut up old greeting cards to glue onto the box. The decorations will remind you of the people who cared and sent you a card.

◎ Write the letters for JOY on your box with glue, then sprinkle glitter or sequins on it.

God's Love Fills Me With Truth

Memory Verse

Whoever drinks the water I give him will never thirst. Indeed, the water I give him will become in him a spring of water welling up to eternal life.–John 4:14

Woman at the Well

An extraordinary meeting took place at a well. Jesus asked a Samaritan woman for water. Jews never spoke to Samaritans. Jesus was a Jew. This women was not only a Samaritan, she was involved in bad activities.

She asked why Jesus would talk to her and ask her for water. Jesus used the opportunity to say He could give her "living" water. She did not understand His answer, but it was enough to make her curious.

The woman thought Jesus was a prophet, so she asked where to worship God. Jesus explained that it is how, not where, one worships that matters. He said we must worship in spirit and in truth. Then He told her all about her life even though she had never met Him before and, when asked, told her He was the Messiah.

The woman became excited. She couldn't believe that this was the Messiah — and He was talking to her! She forgot her water jug and ran to tell others to come and meet Jesus, asking, "Could this be the Christ?"

What excites you about Jesus? Make this well as a reminder to seek truth and to be a person who tells others about Jesus.

Prayer

Jesus, fill me with truth. Help me discover more about You through reading Your Word. Amen.

Dazzling Thoughts

◎ A well is made to draw water out of the ground. God's Word stored in your heart will be a place to draw out thoughts of Him.

◎ In Psalm 42:1-2, the psalmist speaks of thirsting for God as a deer thirsts for water. Think about how you feel about wanting to know God.

◎ People dig deep to make a well. Digging into God's Word means to think and explore what it means.

◎ When water is pumped from a well it gushes out like a river. When someone asks a Christian about Jesus, the words should flow out like a river, too. And they will if her heart is filled with words of God!

 Journaling

I need water for lots of things like: _____

_____

_____

_____

I need God's Word, too. God's Word helps me: _____

_____

_____

_____

A well is dug deep, so in times of drought, there will still be

water. If I memorize Bible words, they can "pour" into my mind

to help me. The verse I remember most when things go wrong

is: _____

_____

_____

_____

_____

Cool Craft! Bible Verse Well

What You'll Need:

* empty pint-size milk or juice carton
* brown and gray paper
* scissors
* glue
* aluminum foil

What To Do:

1. Cut the carton to look like a well as shown at right by slicing open the top and leaving four "posts."

2. Rip or cut brown and gray paper into circular shapes that look like stones.

3. Glue the paper stones onto the well. Overlap them.

4. Cut a 4" x 4½" rectangle of poster board. Fold it in half. Glue the rectangle on top of the carton well for a roof.

5. Cut and glue a piece of foil in the bottom of the well to look like water. You can cover the inner side wall of the well with foil, too.

6. Cut paper into rectangles that fit in the well. On one side, write the address (reference) of a Bible verse that you like. On the other side write out the words of the verse.

7. As you learn a verse, drop it in the well. The well will fill up with verses to show how your heart is also filling up with God's Word.

Sparkling Ideas

◎ Glue glitter or silver sequins inside the well to make it sparkle. Think of how Jesus makes your life sparkle.

◎ Glue a mirror in the bottom of the well. Just as a mirror shines a reflection, if you live God's Word you will mirror God's love in your life.

◎ Use a white liquid correction pen to outline the stones of the well, making it look like the cement that holds the rocks together.

◎ In the Bible, people named the wells they made. The names referred to what happened at the location of the well. Look up these wells in the Bible (parentheses tell what the names mean):

- Beer Lahai Roi – ("the well of the living one who sees me") Genesis 16:7-14
- Beersheba –("the well of the oath") – Genesis 21:30-31
- Esek – ("strife") – Genesis 26:20
- Rehoboth – ("broad places and streets") – Genesis 26:22

◎ Think of a name for the well you made. Write it on the roof of the well.

53

God's Love Fills Me With Music

Memory Verse

In front are the singers, after them the musicians; with them are the maidens playing tambourines. –Psalm 68:25

Solomon's Bride

Does a big parade with singers and musicians sound like fun? This one in Psalms describes a worship assembly. The people gathered to praise God. The maidens (young, unmarried girls) played tambourines as part of the worship.

The parade was held to celebrate King David's victory in bringing the ark of the covenant to Mt. Zion, a high hill in Jerusalem. God chose this hill for His dwelling place.

Psalm 68 begins with the words Moses used when the Israelites started moving toward the Promised Land. This psalm celebrated the completion of that journey — more than 400 years after Moses had started it!

Have you ever taken a long trip? When you travel do you feel excited as you arrive at the right place? Has God arrived at the right place in your life? God needs to be set high above all else, in the center of your life and your heart.

Make this tambourine bracelet to celebrate and worship God. Take time to celebrate God's presence, whether you are alone, with friends or at church. Use music in your celebration!

Prayer

Thank You, Father, for Your presence in my life. Help me to keep You in the center of my life. Amen.

✳ Dazzling Thoughts ✳

- ◎ Psalm 68:19 says, "Praise be to the Lord, to God our Savior, who daily bears our burdens." You can praise God when things go wrong because God is still in control.

- ◎ A tambourine is a shallow drum with jingling discs. It can be shaken or hit with the hand.

- ◎ A tambourine is the first instrument mentioned in the Bible, in Genesis 31:27. It is also the first instrument played in the Bible, in Exodus 15:20.

 Journaling

The longest trip I ever took was: _____

_____

When I arrived I felt: _____

_____

Jesus is always with me. Jesus said so in Matthew 28:20! Jesus

kept me safe on a trip when: _____

_____

_____

In Psalm 150, all sorts of instruments are used to praise God.

My favorite is: _____

I can keep God at the center of my life today by: _____

_____

Cool Craft! Tambourine Bracelet

What You'll Need:

* jingle bells
* plastic needlepoint canvas
* needlepoint yarn or metallic cord
* needlepoint needle
* scissors

What To Do:

1. Wrap the plastic canvas around your wrist and measure

how much is needed to make a bracelet that can <u>slip over</u> <u>your hand.</u>

2. Cut the plastic canvas six holes wide. It should also be three holes longer than the bracelet length you measured.

3. Overlap the three end holes and stitch them together with the needle and yarn, sewing in and out of the overlapped holes. Tie a knot on the inside to form a seam.

4. Starting at the seam and using a long piece of yarn, make an overcast stitch around the edge of the bracelet. To make an overcast stitch, go in top of each hole, around the edge of the canvas, under the bottom and into the next hole.

5. Edge the other side using the same overcast stitch but add a jingle bell at every fifth hole. Slide the needle through the jingle bell, and up to the edge of the bracelet, allowing the bells to dangle at the edge.

Sparkling Ideas

◎ Make rhythm with the tambourine. Play it while listening to your favorite praise tape. Use it on your wrist or off, tapping it against your palm. Experiment making different sounds with the tambourine. Try dancing while using it.

◎ Decorate the bracelet, using glue, sequins, buttons or felt cutouts.

◎ Stitch needlepoint designs on the bracelet, or stitch your name. Look at a needlepoint book for ideas and patterns.

◎ Make several bracelets for your church Sunday school class or a preschool.

◎ Read Psalm 150 and think about how making joyful music praises God.

◎ Make tambourine bracelets and use them to carol for senior citizens or neighbors.

◎ Read Psalm 150 and think about how making joyful music praises God.

◎ Here are some needlepoint patterns to stitch on your bracelet:

God's Love Teaches Me How to Love

Memory Verse

So, as those who have been chosen of God, holy and beloved, put on a heart of compassion, kindness, humility, gentleness, and patience. –Colossians 3:12 NASB

Persis

Paul sent greetings to many believers. In Romans 16:12, Paul wrote, "Greet my dear friend Persis…who has worked very hard in the Lord." It is the only mention of Persis in the Bible.

Yet these few words tell quite a bit about her. Only three people in Rome received an endearing description from Paul. In some Bible translations, Paul called this woman "the beloved."

Paul praised Persis for working hard for God. Many people work at being good Christians but not all reflect God's love as they work. Persis so sparkled with love that she was dear to others. She received love because she gave love. In praising her, Paul reminded people of reasons to praise someone.

Paul, in a different letter, spoke of those who are beloved. He commented on their hearts, filled with kindness and other virtues. These virtues cause a person to be loved by others.

Make this heart mobile as a reminder that love should move us into an action that reflects His love. Remember to praise those who are beloved to God.

Prayer

God, teach me to love and put love into action. Help me to be a beloved disciple. Amen.

Dazzling Thoughts

◎ Yarn ties the mobile together. Love ties us to God and other Christians.

◎ Wind moves the hearts on the mobile. God's Holy Spirit moves people's hearts.

◎ The mobile hearts hang from a plate. Food is served on a plate but love comes from God and is shown in serving others.

◎ Look up Bible verses about hearts. Write them on the hearts of the mobile. Here are some to read: 1 Samuel 16:7; Proverbs 17:22; Matthew 5:8; Matthew 11:29; Romans 10:10; and Ephesians 5:19.

 Journaling

God's love makes me: _____

_____

_____

The one virtue in the memory verse I need to work on is: _____

_____

I can work on it by: _____

_____

_____

_____

Many different hearts on the mobile remind me that there is a

lot to learn about love. One person who loves me is: _____

_____

That person shows he or she loves me by: _____

_____

_____

I can show my love by: _____

_____

Cool Craft! Heart Mobile

What You'll Need:

* paper plate
* construction paper or craft foam
* white yarn
* aluminum foil
* colored cellophane
* hole punch
* scissors
* glue
* markers

What To Do:

1. The bottom of the plate will form the top of the mobile.

2. Cut three hearts from paper or foam. Cut a heart shape from the centers of all three.

3. The first one is your open heart. Read Acts 16:14. Write on the heart: "Be open to God's love."

4. For the second one, cut a foil heart and glue it over the center opening. Read John 13:35. Write: "Reflect God's love on it."

5. For the third one, cut a cellophane heart and glue it over the opening. Read Romans 12:2. Remember, God's love colors your life and transforms your thoughts. Write: "God's love colors me." (To make the filled hearts prettier, sandwich the foil or cellophane between two hearts.)

6. Cut out a solid heart, then cut out gradually smaller hearts and glue them on top of the larger heart, making a target. Read 1 John 4:7. Write: "Be filled with God's love."

7. Cut out a heart and punch holes in it to form a lacy-looking heart. Read Matthew 5:16. Write: "Let God's love shine through you!"

8. To make the hanger, punch three holes, equally spaced, on the inside edge of the plate (see diagram). String one length of yarn through each hole. Tie a knot inside the plate for each length. Tie the other ends of these lengths together to form hanger.

9. To add the string heart-hangers: String the ends of a length of yarn down through two holes (see diagram). At the end of each piece, attach one of the hearts you made by punching a hole in the top of each one. When hanging the mobile you can vary the height of the hearts by pulling on the yarn and taping it on the top of the plate.

❋ ❋ ❋ ❋ ❋ ❋ ❋ ❋
❋ **Sparkling Ideas** ❋
❋ ❋ ❋ ❋ ❋ ❋ ❋ ❋ ❋

◎ Make more hearts to add to the mobile. Blow ink or paint through a straw on one heart. Remember that each person's life will form a beautiful pattern in God's eyes.

◎ Use an eyedropper and paint a heart to make a blotto painting. Remember that Jesus shed His blood to give us life. Death turned into beauty!

◎ Decorate a heart with stickers as a reminder to "stick" with Jesus always.

◎ A purple heart represents royalty or courage. Jesus, our King, showed courage in dying for us. Think about the other colors for hearts.

◎ As a reminder to follow the memory verse, make these virtue hearts:

Kindness

Glue on a penny as a reminder to be giving in little things, too.

Gentleness

Glue on a cotton ball as a reminder to be as soft and gentle as a lamb.

Humility

Draw a foot or hand as a reminder to serve others.

Patience

Draw a little clock as a reminder to wait for others.

Compassion

Make a foil teardrop on one side and a smile on the other as a reminder to share feelings, cry or laugh with the other person.

God's Love Answers My Needs

Memory Verse

She gave this name to the Lord who spoke to her: "You are the God who sees me," for she said, "I have now seen the One who sees me." –Genesis 16:13

Hagar

Hagar, a slave woman, spoke these words. Abraham's wife, Sarah, owned Hagar. Sarah tried to use Hagar to bring about God's promise of a son for Abraham, but it wasn't God's answer or God's timing.

After she became pregnant, Hagar stopped liking Sarah. Sarah felt angry and hurt, so she mistreated Hagar, who fled to the desert. She stopped by a spring where she heard an angel. The angel didn't help Hagar escape but told her to return and obey Sarah. The angel knew of Hagar's pregnancy and told her to name her baby Ishmael, which means "God hears." The angel also told Hagar that her son would start a nation.

Years later, Sarah and Hagar fought again. Sarah sent Hagar and Ishmael away to the desert. Hagar cried. The angel spoke to Hagar again, and God helped Hagar by providing water in the desert.

Problems can make us better people if we turn to God for help. By praying, we build a better relationship with God to keep us from stumbling over the same things again and again. Make this prayer block and use it to build your ties with God.

Prayer

Dear Lord, I want to listen to You speak. When I feel hurt or mistreated, help me listen and do what is right. In times of trouble, help me trust You. Amen.

Dazzling Thoughts

◎ God always listens. He listened to Hagar cry, even though she wasn't actually praying. But God prefers that you pray to Him. After all, how would you like it if no one ever talked to you and you only got to listen in on other people's conversations?

◎ Four important parts to prayer include praising God, asking for forgiveness, thanking Him for all He does and asking Him to help. Choose to put words and pictures on the Prayer Block as reminders of the four parts of prayer.

◎ The pictures on the block are prayer reminders. When you pray, picture your day and picture Bible stories that come to your mind. These stories are God's words, so think about them and reread them.

 # Journaling

Sometimes I can't think of what to say to God. My mind is

blocked. That's the time when I should think about what I read

in my Bible. Today, I read: _____

_____

_____

_____

Praise means to show love for God and who God is. Here's my

praise for God today: _____

_____

_____

_____

I need forgiveness when I do wrong. God, forgive me for: ____

_____

_____

God blesses me every day. Thank You, God, for: _____

_____

God loves me and wants to help me. Lord, please help me: _____

_____

I will help _____

with _____

_____

_____

Cool Craft! Prayer Blocks

Wood Prayer Block

What You'll Need:

* wooden block
* stickers
* permanent markers
* old magazines
* sandpaper
* scissors
* glue
* paintbrush
* bowl
* water

What To Do:

1. Sand the block until it is smooth.

2. Decorate each side of the block with stickers, drawings, words or cut-out pictures.

3. Mix equal amounts of water and glue. Paint the block with the mixture. Let the sides and top dry before painting the bottom. This "decoupages" the block, making it shiny and protecting the decorations. Or you can spray the block with a spray decoupage.

Photo Block

What You'll Need:

* plastic photo block
* white cardboard or gift wrap
* scissors
* glue
* tape

What To Do:

1. Take out the cardboard inside the block. Cover it with paper.
2. Decorate each side with pictures or words.
3. Place the covered block inside the plastic block.

Sparkling Ideas

◎ If you make the photo block, you can tape the pictures with double-sided tape so you can vary the pictures and make a new prayer block!

◎ Keep the prayer block beside your bed as a reminder to pray and what to say. Pray when you wake and before you sleep.

◎ If you are not sure what you want to pray for, "roll" the prayer block and pray for whatever comes out on top!

◎ Make prayer blocks for children in your church nursery or in a mission.

◎ Mix clear glitter with the glue and water. The block will sparkle!

◎ Try these pictures as reminders of four important parts of prayer:

• A globe to praise God for creating everything and being in control of all.

• A cross to remember Jesus died for you and wants to forgive your sins.

• Your photo to remember to thank God for life and so much more!

• Lips to remember to ask God for help for others and for your needs.

Aglow with Crafts

Celebrate **beauty,**

beautiful friends,

beautiful smiles

and **beautiful** handiwork.

In this section you will celebrate inner and outer beauty. From a poor widow to a beautiful queen, find out what real beauty means. Make crafts to wear that also hold messages about God. When people compliment you on your handiwork, use it to witness about women in the Bible. From barrettes that crown your head to decorated sneakers, have fun being creative and celebrate the beautiful you that God created!

God Created Me with Care

Memory Verse

Adam named his wife Eve, because she would become the mother of all the living. –Genesis 3:20

Eve

The word Eve means "life." God created Eve to be the mother of all people. Eve became a nurturer to all children, animals and plants. A mother takes tender care of her babies. That is how God wanted Eve to care for all the life He created. When God created her, He created someone who could give love and care for others.

The Bible does not tell us exactly how Eve treated God's creations. God does not tell us exactly how to do everything. He lets us learn and discover. Think of your own mother. How does she care for you? How does she show her love?

Do you ever think about how you treat God's creations? Do you take time to look at animals God made and marvel at how He made so many types with different abilities? Stop and look at all God made. Take time to feed animals and water plants. Think of ways to help protect them.

Make these animal pins as a reminder of all God created and to think about caring for God's creations.

Prayer

Lord, thank You for taking care in making me. Help me take care of the world You made, especially the people and animals. Amen.

Dazzling Thoughts

◎ We can learn from the animals God made. Think about it!

◎ Look up these Bible verses about animals: Psalm 104 and Proverbs 30:24-31.

◎ Look at animals in a new way, like seeing butterfly wings as pages!

Journaling

My favorite animal that God made is: _____

I think God made that animal because it teaches people that: _____

_____

_____

A pin attaches near my heart and stays close to me. I can keep

close to God by: _____

_____

_____

_____

_____

Cool Craft! Animal Heart Pins

What You'll Need:

* two wood or craft foam hearts
* white paint
* two pin backs
* jewelry glue
* white craft foam
* markers
* two 10 mm wiggle eyes
* one chenille stem
* scissors

What To Do:
Bunny Pin

1. Paint white a 2½" heart or cut a heart from white craft foam.

2. Cut bunny ears from the white foam. Color the centers pink.

3. Turn the heart upside-down with the point at the top.

4. Glue the bunny ears at the top of pin, on the back, one on either side of the point.

5. Glue on or draw eyes.

6. Glue a pink pompom where the heart dips.

7. Draw on black whiskers.

8. Cut a tiny tongue from foam. Color it red. Glue it at the bottom of the face, on the backside.

9. Glue on the pin back.

Butterfly Pin

1. Paint a 2½" heart a light color.

2. Decorate the heart as desired. Try to make the two sides of the heart match. These are the butterfly's wings.

3. Starting 4" from one end, wrap a chenille stem around a pencil. Stop 2" from the other end. Slide the chenille stem off the pencil.

4. Lay the curled part of the chenille stem down the center of the heart with the straight part hanging over the point of the heart. Bring the 4-inch straight piece up the backside of the heart. Twist the two ends together. Then curl the ends to form the antennae. If the curly part is too loose, scrunch it up.

5. Glue the pin back on the back side, lengthwise, next to the chenille stem.

✻ Sparkling Ideas

◎ Design and make other animal pins. Sketch hearts, then doodle around them to create animals.

◎ Make bunny pins for friends at Easter. On the back of each heart write, "Somebunny loves you. Jesus does."

◎ Buy different sizes of hearts to make baby and mother animal pins.

◎ Make magnets by gluing a magnet instead of a pin to the heart back.

◎ Cut hearts from plastic lids. Color the plastic with permanent markers.

God Surrounds Me with Family

Memory Verse

"I am the Lord's servant," Mary answered. *"May it be to me as you have said." Then the angel left her.* –Luke 1:38

Mary

Mary never entered a beauty pageant and wasn't born rich or in a palace, yet God chose her as the most special of women: to be Jesus' mother. Mary did not think of herself as more important than other people even after the angel spoke. Instead, she called herself a servant of the Lord and focused on God. Mary rejoiced in God and felt happy to be used to glorify Him.

Mary carried Jesus in her womb and gave birth to Him. Jesus was tied to Mary, attached by the umbilical cord. More importantly, God's love united Mary and Jesus as mother and child. God also gave Jesus an earthly father, Joseph, Mary's husband, to complete the family.

Each person has the opportunity to be tied to Jesus forever, united in love. Each person can respond to God with willingness to do His will, as Mary did. Have you chosen to be united to Jesus forever? If not, stop and ask Jesus into your heart. Make this knotted belt as a reminder to stay tied to Jesus.

Prayer

Lord Jesus, I believe in You and ask You to be my Lord and Savior. Amen.

Dazzling Thoughts

◎ Proverbs 31 describes a wise woman. In verse 24 the woman is praised for selling belts to tradesmen, as well as selling garments she makes. Learning crafts can help girls and women be more versatile and earn money.

◎ The armor of God includes wearing a belt of truth (Ephesians 6:14). Read what Jesus said about truth in John 8:32.

◎ A rope is strengthened when twisted with other ropes. There is strength in numbers. You are stronger with Jesus. Read Philippians 4:13.

Journaling

Being tied to Jesus by love is great because: _____

_____

_____

Proverbs 6:21 says, "Bind them [God's commandments] upon your heart forever; fasten them around your neck." God wants me to keep His word in my heart. I can do this by: _____

_____

_____

_____

_____

A belt holds up pants and skirts. Jesus holds me up. I remember when Jesus helped me: _____

_____

_____

_____

_____

✳ ✳ ✳ ✳ ✳ ✳ ✳ ✳ ✳

Cool Craft! Knotted Belt

What You'll Need:

* measuring tape
* craft cord
* beads
* scissors

What To Do:

1. Measure your waist. Multiply the number by 4 to get the length of cord you need. Cut three cords that are that length.

2. Tie the cords together at one end. Leave a few inches of cord on the end so you can tie the belt later when you wear it.

3. Using the two outside cords, make three square knots (see how to make a square knot on the next page) around the middle cord.

4. String a bead onto the middle cord and push it next to the last square knot.

5. Repeat steps 3 and 4 until your belt is the desired length. Leave a few inches of cord on the end. Tie the ends together.

Note: This uses about one bead per inch. To use fewer beads, tie more square knots before stringing on the beads.

Square Knots

To form square knots, always keep the same thread on top. Pass the left cord in front of the middle cord and out behind the right cord, leaving a loop to the left of

the middle cord. Take the right cord over the left cord, behind the middle cord and up through the loop. Pull the two outer cords to tighten them. This is a half knot. To finish the square knot, reverse the directions by bringing the right cord in front of the middle cord.

Sparkling Ideas

◎ To make a twist or spiral of knots, make a series of half knots, always bringing the left cord in front of the middle cord. Try making a twist belt instead of a square knot belt.

◎ Use three different colors of cord to make a rainbow belt.

◎ String different colors of beads to form a pattern.

◎ Use colored beads to create a message:

red: love or blood	yellow: light
purple: royalty	blue: heaven
white: purity or sheep	brown: wheat or bread
black: death or the cross	
green: growth or the eternal God	
gold: crown , wheat seed or salvation	
silver: the cost of temptation	
orange: the flame of the Holy Spirit	

God Created My Inner Beauty

Memory Verse

Now the king was attracted to Esther more than to any of the other women, and she won his favor and approval more than any of the other virgins. So he set a royal crown on her head and made her queen instead of Vashti. –Esther 2:17

Esther

Esther, an orphan, found favor with a king and became queen. It sounds like a fairy tale but this happened because Esther's inner beauty shone through.

Inner beauty begins with obedience.

Mordecai took care of Esther, his niece, after her parents died. Esther obeyed Mordecai, even when obeying him meant she might die.

The penalty for approaching the king in the inner court without being invited was death, unless the king held out his royal scepter. To save her people, the Jews, Mordecai told Esther to talk with the king. Queen Esther asked her people to fast (to not eat) for three days. She also fasted, then approached the king.

The king handed his scepter to Esther and spared her life. Esther asked him to dinner twice before asking him to help her people. He ordered the enemy of the Jews to be killed and found a way to save all her people.

Decorate hair combs as little crowns. Each time you wear one remember a queen who cared more for her people than for her own life.

Prayer

Lord, help me be obedient to You and the people You put in authority over me. Help me to place the needs of other people before my own needs. Amen.

Dazzling Thoughts

◎ Long hair can be a source of joy and pride for women. Look this up in 1 Corinthians 11:15.

◎ Let your hair remind you of God's love. Jesus said, "And even the very hairs of your head are all numbered." (Matthew 10:30)

◎ A comb untangles snarls. When people lie, they make a tangle of words. Jesus forgives people and helps untangle problems.

◎ "Comb" also means "to search thoroughly." Comb the scriptures to discover new things.

Journaling

I can change my hair style. I can let my hair grow, or cut it.

What I like best about my hair is: _____

_____

_____

It's awesome that God numbers my hairs because: _____

_____

_____

_____

My favorite hair style is: _____

_____

When I combed the Bible, I discovered this verse: _____

_____

_____

_____

✳ ✳ ✳ ✳ ✳ ✳ ✳ ✳ ✳

Cool Craft! Decorated Hair Comb

What You'll Need:

❋ plastic hair comb
❋ star-shaped wood cutouts, assorted sizes
❋ star sequins or stickers
❋ acrylic paint or spray paint

What To Do:

1. Paint the stars all one color or a few different colors.

2. Arrange the stars across the comb and find the arrangement you like best.

3. Glue the wooden stars onto the top of the comb.

4. Glue star sequins onto the wooden stars.

Sparkling Ideas

◎ For a marble effect, paint the stars blue, then sponge paint them with pale blue or white.

◎ Instead of wooden shapes, glue sea shells on your comb.

◎ Tie ribbons on the comb before gluing on the stars. Then you'll have stars and stripes!

God Created Plans for My Life

Memory Verse

But Joshua spared Rahab the prostitute, with her family and all who belonged to her, because she hid the men Joshua had sent as spies to Jericho — and she lives among the Israelites to this day. –Joshua 6:25

Rahab

A little hospitality saved a family. Rahab welcomed spies into her home, hid them and helped them escape. In return, the spies promised to save Rahab and her family if she tied a red ribbon in her window.

Rahab and all her people had heard about the God of the Israelites. They knew the power of God who opened the Red Sea, saved His people and destroyed their enemies. Rahab showed her faith when she said, "The Lord your God is God in heaven above and on the earth below" (Joshua 2:11).

Rahab's people feared the Israelites, yet she protected them and trusted godly people to respond with kindness. The spies agreed, and spared her and her family. God rewarded Rahab's actions and faith. An Israelite named Salmon married Rahab and she lived with the Israelites the rest of her life. God even chose her to be an ancestor of Jesus. It began with trust and a red ribbon!

Weave red ribbons in your hair as a reminder that faith and kindness are threads that bind people to God.

Prayer

Lord, help me show hospitality and kindness to others. Help me to trust in Your saving power. Amen.

- ◎ The Bible tells us to "Offer hospitality to one another without grumbling." (1 Peter 4:9)

- ◎ Rahab used a scarlet, or red, ribbon. Red is a color used for love, for the sacrifice of blood and for sins (Isaiah 1:18). Rahab, a sinner, sacrificed her safety by hiding the spies. In the end, she received safety and love with marriage to one of the Israelites.

- ◎ Hospitality contains the word "hospital." We can provide a place for healing when we open our home and our heart to those who need it. Sometimes it is hard to be hospitable to someone who is not nice or fun. In those cases, we need to offer love and the healing of Christ.

※ ※ ※ ※ ※ ※ ※ ※ ※

 Journaling

A hospitable home is where people feel welcomed. To help

others feel welcomed in my home or my room I can: _____

_____

_____

_____

_____

One time it was hard to be hospitable was: _____

_____

_____

_____

_____

I can be hospitable by: _____

_____

_____

_____

_____

I can add a red ribbon to my room to remind me to be

hospitable. I'll put it: _____

_____

Cool Craft! Ribbons and Braids

What You'll Need:

✳ ribbons
✳ beads
✳ hair bands, barrettes or pony tail bands

What To Do:

1. Fold a ribbon in half and attach it to a hair decoration with a larkshead knot (see diagram). To do this, put the loop of the fold about an inch above the item. Bring the ends around the other side of the item and through the loop. Pull to tighten. You can also add the ribbon directly to a lock of hair with a larkshead knot.

2. Slide on a bead and make a knot below the bead. Add beads at various places on the ribbons, securing each with a knot.

   Choose bead colors to tell a message:

   White: Jesus was a baby, pure and holy
   Green: the child Jesus, who grew in grace as the Son of God

Blue: the baptism of Jesus in the river Jordan

Yellow: the light of truth that Jesus gave in His teachings

Red: the blood Jesus shed out of love for each of us

Black: Jesus' death on the cross

Purple: King Jesus, who now sits on a heavenly throne

Orange: the Holy Spirit that Jesus sent to guide us in our life

3. Attach the ribbon to your hair by tying it on a hair band, barrette or pony tail band. Let the ribbon hang or braid it into your hair. To braid, use three pieces of hair, and add a ribbon to two of the pieces. Braid as normal.

Sparkling Ideas

◎ Attach two ribbons together.

◎ Make a ribbon headband. Braid three ribbons together, long enough to reach from behind one ear to behind the other ear. Add elastic to both ends to make the headband fit.

◎ Coordinate the ribbons with your clothes and add ribbons to your clothing. Tie several matching ribbons together in bows and pin on your outfit.

◎ Curl the ribbons with a curling iron.

◎ Use plastic lacing instead of ribbon. Curl it by wrapping it around a pencil and dipping it in hot water.

God Surrounds Me with Beautiful Words

Memory Verse

He [Apollos] began to speak boldly in the synagogue. When Priscilla and Aquila heard him, they invited him to their home and explained to him the way of God more adequately. –Acts 18:26

Priscilla

Priscilla and her husband knew the importance of listening. Paul stayed with this couple and traveled with them. They shared a profession, as tent-makers, with Paul. Working together gave Priscilla and Aquila an opportunity to listen and learn from Paul. Listening is the beginning of being a disciple.

Priscilla and Aquila also listened to another man, Apollos, preach about Jesus. He knew little about Jesus and only preached about the baptism of John. Rather than publicly correct Apollos, this couple invited him into their home and privately taught him about Jesus. Apollos listened. He believed what he heard and told others. He became a great preacher and defender of the faith.

In their home, Priscilla and Aquila also established a church, one noted by Paul. This couple continually opened their home, their hearts and their ears to other people.

Make love bug earrings and work at becoming a love bug, a person who listens and responds with love. Remember that when people say something wrong to talk to them in private and not embarrass them.

Prayer

Lord, help me be a good listener. Help me learn to teach others in a loving way about Jesus. Amen.

Dazzling Thoughts

- ◎ Love bugs always travel in pairs, flying together. When you are united with Jesus, He always travels with you.

- ◎ In friendship, what keeps friends close is listening to one another. God always listens to your prayer, but do you listen to Him? Do you listen to His Word?

- ◎ Hearing the gospel is important. Let your love bug earrings remind you to tell others about Jesus.

- ◎ "And you also were included in Christ when you heard the word of truth, the gospel of your salvation. Having believed, you were marked in Him with a seal, the promised Holy Spirit." Ephesians 1:13

 Journaling

The Bible says in Proverbs 6:6 to observe the ant and be wise.

An ant works hard and prepares for the future. I can prepare

for my future by: _____

_____

_____

_____

_____

God gave me two ears but only one mouth because: _____

_____

_____

_____

I'm happy Jesus is always with me because: _____

_____

_____

_____

God made my friends, too. I love my friend: _____

What I like best about my friend is: _____

_____

_____

Cool *Craft!* Love Bug Earrings

What You'll Need:

* ❋ body and wing patterns on page 96
* ❋ two 1" wooden hearts
* ❋ white paper
* ❋ black craft foam
* ❋ lace scraps
* ❋ beads or sequins
* ❋ earring backings
* ❋ jewelry glue
* ❋ red paint
* ❋ black permanent marker
* ❋ white thread

What To Do:

1. Paint the hearts red. When they are dry, turn them upside down so the painted side is still up but the point is at the top.

2. Trace the body and wing patterns on white paper. Using the left pattern, cut two shapes from black craft foam. Glue one shape to the back of each heart. These are the legs.

3. Create the eyes by gluing beads or sequins on the heart.

4. Draw a mouth.

5. Use the second pattern to cut wings from lace. Tie the lace across the center to gather it.

6. Glue the wings to the backs of the hearts.

7. Glue an earring backing to each.

✳ Sparkling Ideas ✳

◎ Make love bug earrings for a friend.

◎ Add glitter to the tips of the wings.

◎ Paint the hearts other colors for a variety of love bugs.

◎ Make matching love bug pins or button covers using supplies from the craft store.

◎ Make love bugs as a gift for someone who listens to you and your problems.

◎ Make honey bees with black and yellow markers, using a wooden oval shape. Give them to people who teach you about God's Word ("sweeter than honey," Psalm 19:10) and remind you to say pleasant words (Proverbs 16:24).

God Created a New Heart in Me

Memory Verse

"I tell you the truth," he said, "this poor widow has put in more than all the others. All these people gave their gifts out of their wealth; but she out of her poverty put in all she had to live on."
–Luke 21:3-4

A Widow

Jesus watched a certain widow drop a few copper coins into the offering. She gave a tiny amount yet Jesus praised her because He understood her sacrifice.

We can feel the compassion of Jesus in His words. "Compassion" means to understand someone's suffering. Jesus knew that giving money was more difficult for this woman than just skipping a meal or putting off buying new clothes. Jesus said that the coins were all the money she had to live on. Her cupboards were bare and her pockets were empty, yet she gave to God, putting her life in God's care. That's the best place to put troubles!

The Bible doesn't tell us if God helped this poor widow or blessed her with wealth, yet God promises to care for our needs. God knew her needs and He knows your needs, too.

Make this stained glass window T-shirt as a reminder that a heart is an open window. God looks in and understands our deepest needs. Remember to tell God your needs. He'll always understand.

Prayer

Lord, search my heart and help fill it with love for You. Help me be generous. All that I am and have I offer to You, Lord. Amen.

Dazzling Thoughts

◎ Stained glass is colored glass. The light can shine through it but the light is colored as if passing through a filter. This is how God's love colors your life. Your life might look the same as someone else's, but with God you see things differently.

◎ The throne of God is described in the Bible as having a sea of glass, like crystal, in front of it. Nothing is hidden from the throne. Even the floor is glass. Read about the throne in Revelations 4:1-11.

◎ The tape covers the T-shirt and does not allow the paint to pass through. Jesus protects us from temptation and keeps sin from entering our lives.

 # Journaling

Mixing colors to make a painting is fun. The colors swirl and make me think of: _____

_____

_____

_____

I want to be a window for God where people can look into my life and see Jesus through me. I can do this by: _____

_____

_____

_____

I want to be generous like the poor widow. I can give God my time by: _____

_____

and share my talents by: _____

_____

Cool Craft! Hearts of Glass T-Shirts

What You'll Need:

* plain T-shirt
* four fabric paints
* ¼" wide quilter's tape
* 1" wide masking tape
* paint brush
* large piece of cardboard

What To Do:

1. Place the cardboard inside the T-shirt to prevent the paint from bleeding through.

2. Tuck the sleeves inside the back of the T-shirt or pin them to the back.

3. Use the masking tape to make a heart outline on the front of the T-shirt.

4. Use the quilter's tape to make divisions in the heart by cutting assorted lengths of tape and placing them in the heart, making sure the ends meet the edge or another piece of tape. The tape will be like the lead strips in a stained glass window. These will remain white (or the color of your T-shirt) when removed.

5. Paint all of the open spaces in the heart. Overlap the colors, using two to four colors in each space. Swirl paints together or just dab colors beside each other.

6. Let the paint dry, then remove the tape and the cardboard.

7. When your shirt needs to be washed after you have worn it, be sure to pull it inside out and hang it up to drip dry. This will protect the paint from peeling or bleeding.

Sparkling Ideas

◎ Make other shapes with tape, such as a cross or fish.

◎ To make "lacy" sleeves, cut from the shoulder to 1" above the lower edge of sleeve in several evenly-spaced places.

◎ When you place the tape to make a stained glass look, try making shaped spaces, such as a cross or initials.

◎ Try glitter paint for a sparkling effect.

◎ Glue fabric beads onto the heart with fabric glue.

God Surrounds Me with Natural Beauty

Memory Verse

One of those listening was a woman named Lydia, a dealer in purple cloth from the city of Thyatira, who was a worshiper of God. The Lord opened her heart to respond to Paul's message.
–Acts 16:14

Lydia

Lydia sold purple fabric. Purple was a symbol of royalty. Only rich people bought purple fabric. Lydia helped people to be fashionable, yet she was also known as a worshipper of God. Business never kept her from Him. When Paul came to town to preach about God, she stopped and listened.

In response to Lydia's faithfulness, God opened her heart to Paul's words. Lydia and her household were baptized. She then opened her home to Paul and Silas, who stayed with her.

However, Paul's preaching and healing caused problems in the town. The people threw Paul and Silas in jail. Associating with jailed men could hurt a merchant's business. Some people avoided trouble and stayed away from trouble makers.

But Lydia remained faithful. After Paul and Silas were freed from jail they returned to Lydia's home. Paul offered encouragement to the town's believers before he and Silas continued their journey. Lydia discovered the importance of growing as a Christian and being fashioned by God.

Make this fashionable bag with leaf prints as a reminder to grow as a Christian. As a child in God's kingdom you are part of a royal family!

Prayer

Lord, help me grow in wisdom. Help me open my heart to others. Amen.

Dazzling Thoughts

◎ Read 2 Timothy 2:21 about being a vessel or a container that is useful to God. Like an empty bag with room to hold many things, be open to be used by God.

◎ Jesus said that good trees bear good fruit. We need to grow and bear good fruit, the fruits of the Spirit, like joy and peace. Look up the fruits of the Spirit (Galatians 5:22-23).

◎ A leaf is healthy because it gets water, sunlight and soil nutrients. If you are planted in Christ, you get what you need to grow from God's Word, prayer and Christian fellowship.

◎ A print leaves an impression of the original object. When people meet you, they receive an impression of what you are like. Try to leave an impression that reflects Christ.

Journaling

I'm growing closer to God as I learn more about Him. This week
I learned: _____

_____

_____

_____

A Christian who leaves a good impression is: _____

_____

_____

because: _____

_____

_____

When I grow up I want God to use me. Maybe one day I will

become: _____

_____

_____

_____

Cool Craft! Leaf Print Bag

What You'll Need:

* green fabric paints
* black and green fabric markers
* canvas bag
* aluminum foil
* silk or real leaves
* glass cutting board or waxed paper
* paint roller or wooden dowel

What To Do:

1. Line your canvas bag with aluminum foil to prevent the paint from bleeding through.

2. Pour paint on the glass cutting board or waxed paper. Use a brush or roller to create a thin layer of paint that is larger than your biggest leaf.

3. Lay the spine side of a leaf on the paint. Press or roll over the leaf so it will absorb the paint.

4. Lift the leaf, place it on the bag and press across the leaf with your fingers. Lift off the leaf.

5. Repeat, placing the leaves in various locations. Let the paint dry.

6. After the paint is dry, use markers to add a green vine

connecting the leaves, and black and green to highlight some of the veins in the leaves.

Sparkling Ideas

◎ Try using different sizes of canvas bags. Mini bags are fun for holding candy, pens and pencils or earrings and necklaces.

◎ Stamp paint small grape leaves then paint on clusters of grapes. Use a small pencil eraser to dip paint the grapes.

◎ Make leaves for a family tree and write in your family's names. This makes a great gift!

◎ Use autumn colors of paints for a fall bag.

◎ Make a bag as a gift and fill it with items related to the person's career, hobbies or with Christian symbols.

◎ Create a matching leaf stamp and make stationary to match your bag.

◎ Make a T-shirt to match your bag.

God Created Unity in My Life

Memory Verse

"So may all your enemies perish, O Lord! But may they who love you be like the sun when it rises in its strength." Then the land had peace forty years. –Judges 5:31 (from Deborah's song)

Deborah

Deborah ruled Israel as a judge. She also led her people spiritually. The Israelites lived as slaves under an evil ruler named Sisera. God allowed this problem be-cause the people chose to be evil and disobey God.

God used Deborah to help the people. Deborah instructed Barak to lead a battle that ended in victory for the Israelites and caused the defeat of Sisera. Deborah and Barak worked together, with Deborah giving spiritual guidance and Barak following the advice and leading the people in battle. Deborah united her people and brought peace to the land.

Deborah's strength grew from her faith. Even in song she gave glory to God. God gave Deborah the strength and wisdom to hold her people together as a united nation. She sang words of praise and asked that those who love God be like the sun —

shining and dazzling.

Make this ponytail holder that binds your hair together and decorate it with sparkling beads. Think about how Deborah bound her people together and helped them to be sparkling lights who showed love for God.

Prayer

Lord, help me be a light for others to see You in me. Let my words and deeds shine with Your love. Amen.

◎ This craft is made from recycled soda bottles. God can recycle people, too. Skills used for evil can be used for good!

◎ The ponytail holder is a fish with a fishing pole fastener. Remember that Jesus wants you to "fish" for people. Read Matthew 4:19.

◎ Jesus multiplied fish. You can make many fish ponytail holders to give to other Christians!

◎ When people ask about the fish, use it as an opportunity to talk about Jesus.

 Journaling

The time I talked the most about Jesus was: _____

_____

_____

_____

_____

Deborah received wisdom from God because she spent time

with God. This week I plan to spend _____

time with God.

I can spend time with God reading the Bible, listening to God's

Word, praying, singing praises and listening with my heart. My

favorite time to spend with God is: _____

_____

_____

One time God used me to help someone else was: _____

_____

_____

_____

Cool Craft! Ponytail Holder

What You'll Need:

* plastic soda bottle
* cotton fabric scraps
* spray adhesive or fabric glue
* wooden manicure stick or chopstick
* utility scissors
* fabric scissors
* hole punch

What To Do:

1. Trace the fish shape on page 111 and cut it out.
2. Draw the fish pattern on a plastic bottle and cut it out.
3. Spray glue on both the inside of the plastic fish cut-out and the right side of a fabric scrap that is slightly larger than the fish pattern.
4. Attach the fabric to the plastic fish. Let the glue dry.
5. After the glue has dried, trim the fabric around the fish.
6. Punch a hole at each end of the fish.
7. For a fishing pole, wrap the stick with a piece of string and glue it in place. Or use a marker to draw a fishing line that is wrapped around the "pole." If you are using a chopstick, cut it down to 5½" and sand the end where you cut it.
8. Place the fish over your hair to form a ponytail. Insert the pole into the hole at the fish's mouth, under your hair and out the other hole to fasten it in place.

✳ ✳ ✳ ✳ ✳ ✳ ✳ ✳
Sparkling Ideas
✳ ✳ ✳ ✳ ✳ ✳ ✳ ✳ ✳

◎ Glue sequins on the ponytail holder for fish scales (or just to add sparkle!).

◎ Cut a fin along a curve and bend it out to give the ponytail holder a 3-D look.

◎ Cut other shapes for ponytail holders. Draw them on paper first to make patterns. Coloring books and computer clip art can also be used for patterns.

◎ Make a ponytail holder into a bracelet by tying elastic to the holes and slipping it over your hand.

◎ Make barrettes the same way you make the ponytail holder but stop before you punch the holes. Glue the shape onto a barrette backing.

God's Love Directs My Steps

Memory Verse

The God who made the world and everything in it is the Lord of heaven and earth and does not live in temples built by hands.
–Acts 17:24

Damaris

As Paul arrived in Athens, he was distressed because he saw that the city had a lot of idols. But Paul still found a way to get the people's attention. As he walked around the city he found an idol inscribed to an unknown god. He used this information as a way to evangelize and that changed a woman's life.

The people of Athens took Paul to the Areopagus, which was the court. Paul proclaimed that he was sent to tell them about this unknown god. His words caused some people to believe, including a woman named Damaris. Little is known about Damaris, except that she believed because Paul preached.

The name "Damaris" means "gentle." Paul left Athens soon after speaking there and went on to Corinth. Sometimes a person tells someone about Jesus but never has time to get to know or disciple him or her. Paul trusted God to send others to help Damaris grow as a Christian.

Decorate your sneakers with a rebus (a picture puzzle message) as a reminder to find the gentle souls God loves and to tell them the Good News.

Prayer

Lord, help me tell others about You wherever I go. Amen.

Dazzling Thoughts

◎ It is always the right time to be a good Christian witness. As the Bible says, "How beautiful are the feet of those who bring good news!" (Romans 10:15)

◎ How does someone measure the beauty of feet? If you use your feet to go and tell others about Jesus, to go and help others or to show Christian love, then your feet will be beautiful. People will enjoy hearing your footsteps!

◎ When you hear people coming, stop and pray before speaking to them. Be happy for each person God sends into your life.

◎ Look up these other verses about feet: Psalm 56:13; Psalm 119:105; Isaiah 52:7; Luke 1:79; and Ephesians 6:15.

Journaling

I use my feet in many ways. Today I plan to: _____

_____

_____

_____

I may never be famous. Damaris was only known for one thing.

I'd like to be like Damaris because: _____

_____

_____

_____

The Bible says to prepare my feet with peace. When I go to tell

others about Jesus I need to first have peace in myself because:

_____

_____

_____

_____

Jesus washed the feet of disciples. I can wash the feet of:

_____

_____

Cool Craft! Sneakers with a Message

What You'll Need:

✳ plain tennis shoes with laces
✳ colored beads
✳ fabric paints

What To Do:

1. Paint a Christian rebus on your shoes. To paint the sneakers, you can use fabric markers, stencils, sponge shapes or just paint freehand. The same rebus can be on each sneaker. Or the message can be split with half on each sneaker. Here are two examples of a rebus:

U   R   the      of the   🌎

This is a rebus for "You are the light of the world." Add little plastic jewel "lights" around the sneakers with this rebus.

GGGG   +   US   +   ♡ s   U

This is a rebus for "Jesus loves you." Add little hearts around the sneakers with this rebus as a reminder to share God's love with others. Or write 1's in the hearts and draw stick people as a reminder to love one another!

2. To make a stencil, use heavy plastic, such as bacon packaging. Cut the design with a craft knife, press the design against the sneaker and tape it in place. Then with a sponge dipped in paint, dab the stencil opening. Lift off the stencil when you are done painting. (You might want to try this first on paper to get the hang of it.)

3. String beads onto the laces for another message. Make a rainbow of beads to remember that God put the rainbow in the sky as a sign of His promise.

◎ Draw the design with a disappearing marker before painting. This will help you space the design before painting the permanent design. Use an ink that disappears in 24 hours to make different messages each day!

◎ Have a rebus contest with friends to see who designs the most clever rebus.

◎ Add beads and sequins to your shoes by dropping a circle of paint on a shoe and pushing the bead or sequin into the paint.

◎ Sprinkle glitter on wet paint to add sparkle.

◎ At Christmas time, add jingle bells to laces and make a joyful noise when you walk.

God Surrounds Me with Friends

Memory Verse

Greet Tryphena and Tryphosa, those women who work hard in the Lord. –Romans 16:12

Tryphena and Tryphosa

In the letter to the Romans, Paul sent greetings to over two dozen people, including six women. Two Christian women received a special greeting from Paul with praise for their hard work. He didn't explain what type of work the women did. Their names were Tryphena, which means "delicate," and Tryphosa, which means "dainty." Nothing else is known about the women.

These ladies left a good impression with Paul and other Christians. Because the two women's names were linked together in his greeting, we can guess that they were probably friends. Paul knew the value of working together. He often took a helper with him, and Jesus sent disciples out in pairs. People accomplish more working together than alone. God wants people to work together.

People who are not physically strong or who are shy can be

especially good at nurturing others, showing compassion, gently teaching God's Word and visiting the sick and lonely. Think of how you can work for God. Make two of these doll necklaces. If you are shy, give one to someone as an easy way to make a new friend. If you are not shy, find someone who needs a friend and give her a necklace. Then find a project you can do as a team. Remember that God loves seeing Christians work together!

Prayer

Thank You, Father, for friends. Help me to spend more time with a friend working for You. Amen.

Dazzling Thoughts

◎ The doll necklace reminds you that even a young girl can serve God.

◎ "Let love and faithfulness never leave you; bind them around your neck, write them on the tablet of your heart." (Proverbs 3:3)

◎ The doll necklace can remind you to treat others kindly, as gently as you treat a special doll.

◎ Tryphena and Tryphosa worked together. Oxen are yoked, so they must share the workload evenly. Jesus tells us to take His yoke. Trust Him to always share the burden of your problems. (Matthew 11:29-30)

 Journaling

I like to work with other people, especially with: _____

_____

Something I can do this week with a friend is: _____

_____

_____

_____

It's good to know Jesus helps me and shares my load. That

makes me feel: _____

_____

_____

_____

Having a Christian friend helps: _____

_____

_____

Cool Craft! Doll Necklace

What You'll Need:

* ❋ metallic cord or macramé cord
* ❋ measuring tape or yardstick
* ❋ 1" wooden doll head with hole in center or a plain bead
* ❋ four small jingle bells
* ❋ ½" pom-pom
* ❋ scissors

What To Do:

1. Cut one length of cord that goes around your neck and hangs to whatever necklace length you like.

2. Cut a second piece of cord one yard long.

3. Fold in half the cord you measured around your neck. Three inches from the bottom, fold the second cord around the doubled cord. Make six square knots (see next page) with the shorter cord, continuing to go around the doubled cord. The knots form the doll's body, so be sure to start at the bottom so you can create the arms in the next step.

4. Cut the ends of the knot cord to 3", forming arms.

5. Tie a jingle bell onto the ends of the arms and legs for hands and feet.

6. At the top of the fold of the long cord, slide on the wooden head or bead. Slide it down until it is at the top of the body.

Glue on a pom-pom for hair, or use yarn.

7. If the bead does not have a face, paint it using a toothpick as a brush, or use fine point permanent markers.

Square Knots

To form square knots, always keep the same thread on top. Pass the left cord in front of the middle cord and out behind the right cord, leaving a loop to the left of

the middle cord. Take the right cord over the left cord, behind the middle cord and up through the loop. Pull the two outer cords to tighten them. This is a half knot. To finish the square knot, reverse the directions by bringing the right cord in front of the middle cord.

◎ Add beads on either side of the doll's head.
◎ Use embroidery thread and tiny beads to make dolls on friendship bracelets.
◎ Use a shorter cord to make doll key chains.
◎ Use an overhand knot, instead of a square knot, to form a spiral doll body. This is done by always using the cord on the same side in front of the center cords.
◎ Make doll wreath ornaments for your Christmas tree. After making the doll, cut the cord length to form a 3" loop instead of a long necklace.
◎ Cut half circles of washable felt and glue them on the doll for a skirt.

Beauty to Share

Waterfalls **overflow.**

Water **rushes** out,

splashes and

sparkles in the sunlight.

Love, too, overflows and people see beauty in action. In this section, read about women who supported and fed Jesus, and others who shared wisdom, helped the needy or told others about God. See what made these women sparkle with love and share their time, service, advice and money with others. Have fun making crafts to give away — crafts that will also send a message of love and help you sparkle with love as you give to others. God sees beauty in the lives of all women and girls who look to Him. Let's get "beautiful" God's way!

A Beautiful Believer Brings Joy to Others

Memory Verse

I ask you to receive her [Phoebe] in the Lord in a way worthy of the saints and to give her any help she may need from you, for she has been a great help to many people, including me.
– Romans 16:2

Phoebe

Paul let the Christians in Rome know that a dear friend of his, named Phoebe, planned to come to them. Paul asked the people to accept Phoebe and help her. Why? Because Phoebe had a history of helping other people, including Paul. Phoebe showed her Christian love in the way she lived and reached out to help others. Paul praised Phoebe as a great helper.

It's always good to see someone coming who works hard and helps when there's a project to do. Can you think of someone who always helps you? Would you want other people to treat that friend well? That's what Paul wanted.

To receive someone is to accept and welcome him or her like a guest. Phoebe belonged to the church in Cenchrea, a harbor in

Corinth. Paul called her "our sister" and "a servant of the church." Think of ways to welcome people, especially visitors at your church.

We are to consider other Christians as sisters and brothers. You can serve others and bring joy to children by making these balls of fun that are filled with tiny surprises.

Prayer

Lord, thank You for Christian leaders. I pray for my pastor and my parents, and ask you to show me how I can help them. Amen.

Dazzling Thoughts

- ◎ God gives us little blessings in life. Each day, enjoy all that God made and the surprises He gives you in a sunset or the beauty of nature.

- ◎ Small things can really make a big difference. The Bible talks about the wisdom of four small creatures God made, in Proverbs 30:24-28.

- ◎ The Bible also speaks of moving mountains with only a little faith. Read about that in Matthew 17:20.

- ◎ Mary wrapped Jesus in strips of cloth. He was just a tiny baby, yet He gave us so much!

- ◎ Giving little gifts can be meaningful but so can the gift of little words we say, such as "I love you" or "thank you."

 # Journaling

Paul praised Phoebe and said she helped him. I can help leaders, too. I can: _____

_____

_____

_____

_____

Giving to others can be fun. I remember a time I enjoyed giving was: _____

_____

_____

_____

_____

Something someone said to me today that helped was: _____

_____

_____

_____

_____

I want to remember to be kind and give a gift of joyful words

to others. Today I will: _____

_____

_____

_____

Cool Craft! Balls of Fun

What You'll Need:

❋ crepe paper streamers
❋ tiny toys, stickers or coins
❋ tape

What To Do:

1. Place a tiny "treasure" at one end of a streamer. Begin to roll the streamer into a ball. Turn the paper to crisscross and roll it in more than one direction.

2. Every 6" or so, add another treasure.

3. Continue to roll the ball until all of the tiny treasures are covered inside it or until the ball is the size you want. If your streamer ends before you want it to, just tape another streamer to its end and continue.

4. Tape the end of the streamer to the ball.

❋ ❋ ❋ ❋ ❋ ❋ ❋ ❋ ❋

Sparkling Ideas

◎ Make a Ball of Fun for your mom on Mother's Day. Fill it with earrings, sewing thread, tea bags, Bible verses on love and notes of promises to do household chores.

◎ Make Balls of Fun for children in a hospital. Check first to see what items can be rolled inside the balls.

◎ Make a roll with stickers only and give a sticker booklet with the roll.

◎ Make a verse ball. Roll in separate pieces of paper with the words of a Scripture. If some can be represented by an item, put in the item instead of the word. For example, a flashlight bulb or a birthday candle for "light."

◎ Make several verse balls for a party. Place them in a basket as a decoration. Pass them out during the party and see who solves her or his verse first.

◎ Use the ball as an exchange with a friend. Roll one up for your friend with notes, candies and treasures. Then let your friend reroll it with treasures for you or another friend.

◎ Make Balls of Fun as Easter egg treasures for family or friends.

◎ Send one to a friend who moved away, reminding her that the road between you may be long, but love bridges the distance.

A Beautiful Believer Treasures Life

Memory Verse

But when she could hide him no longer, she got a papyrus basket for him and coated it with tar and pitch. Then she placed the child in it and put it among the reeds along the bank of the Nile. –Exodus 2:3

Jochebed

Jochebed, a Jewish slave, gave birth to a beautiful son. However, Pharaoh, the leader of the Egyptians, gave a command to kill all Jewish baby boys. Jochebed loved her son and hid him as long as possible. But when he was about three months old, it became too hard to hide him anymore. Something else had to be done to save his life.

Jochebed decided to hide Moses in a basket in the river. God did not let Moses die. An Egyptian princess found the baby, adopted him and named him "Moses." But an even more wonderful thing happened: Jochebed was still able to help raise Moses. Miriam, Moses' sister, saw the princess find Moses and offered to find a nurse. Of course, she went straight to her mother, who got to serve as her own son's nurse!

God knows how to give surprise answers to prayer. When we think all is lost, God provides answers. Think of your biggest problem and trust God to provide an answer. Make these little stuffed surprises to remember how God saved a baby who was stuffed in a basket.

Prayer

Lord, thank You for giving me life. Help me treasure all that You created. Amen.

Dazzling Thoughts

◎ God's greatest gift for us is eternal life.

◎ Find out how God wants to bless His children with gifts. Read James 1:17 and Matthew 7:11.

◎ Jesus said that what we treasure reveals what is in our hearts (Matthew 6:21).

◎ Believers can look forward to treasures in heaven (Matthew 19:21).

Journaling

It would be hard to give away something I treasure. My favorite

treasure is: _____

_____

The time God surprised me with a prayer answer was: _____

_____

_____

_____

Some things are hard to do or to let God control. Right now my

biggest problem is: _____

_____

_____

_____

Maybe God sees the answer differently. How else might God

answer my prayer? _____

_____

_____

_____

Cool Craft! Stuffed Treasures

What You'll Need:

* toilet paper roll
* tissue paper or gift wrap
* ribbon
* small gifts to fit inside the roll
* markers
* paper
* scissors

What To Do:

1. Stuff the empty roll with small gifts (some to try: perfume samples, lipstick, toys, pens).

2. Wrap the roll so that the edges of the tissue are 2" longer at both ends.

3. Tie ribbon at the ends of the roll, letting the tissue extend beyond the roll.

4. Decorate the roll with markers. Or try a stencil decoration: Fold paper into a square and then diagonally. Cut according to the pattern on the next page. Unfold and use as a stencil. Wrap the paper around a tube and fill in the spaces with marker. Remove the paper. This stencil has a cross for Jesus, hearts for love and little children to send a message that Jesus loves little children. Think of other stencil messages to design and use!

✳ Sparkling Ideas

- ◉ Fill tubes with items for older people and give them to a nursing home. Items might include small toiletry samples, perfume, lipstick, combs, pens, sugar-free candy or erasers.

- ◉ Use paper towel rolls for larger stuffed treasures. These could even hold magazines!

- ◉ Decorate a tube with stickers.

- ◉ Cover the tubes to match the season, such as red and green for Christmas. Make these as tray favors for nursing homes and children's hospitals.

A Beautiful Believer Receives More Than She Gives

Memory Verse

Then the woman [the widow of Zarephath] said to Elijah, "Now I know that you are a man of God and that the word of the Lord from your mouth is the truth."
– 1 Kings 17:24

The Widow of Zarephath

What a beautiful statement of faith this Scripture is! Yet it took a lot of proof for the widow to proclaim such faith. Elijah performed two miracles for the widow at Zarephath before she was able to make this statement of faith.

This woman felt hopeless when she first met Elijah. She and her son nearly starved to death when Elijah gave her a message from the Lord that her flour and oil would not run out during the drought. She saw God supply flour and oil daily, providing life-giving food.

Yet when the woman's son stopped breathing, she turned and complained to Elijah. Sorrow blinded her faith. Elijah prayed three times and God restored the boy's life. After Elijah's prayer restored her son, the widow made the powerful statement in 1 Kings.

God met her needs. More importantly, God increased her faith. Make a gift topper and think about how the gift of faith belongs at the top of every gift list!

Prayer

Help me trust You, Lord, especially when things are difficult. Thank You for supplying for my needs each day. Amen.

Dazzling Thoughts

◎ Thomas doubted Jesus, but when he saw Him risen from the dead Thomas believed. Jesus said that He blesses those who believe in Him even though they cannot see Him. Believe in Him and read John 20:24-29.

◎ You can fill a gift and wrap it, but only God fills hearts with love.

◎ The best way to top off the day is with prayer and praise.

◎ One little boy gave all he had: five loaves of bread and two small fish. Jesus took the small amount and fed 5,000 people. Give all you have for a few minutes and read John 6:1-14.

Journaling

I first knew Jesus was real when: _____

_____

_____

_____

What Jesus did this week to show His love to me is: _____

_____

_____

_____

_____

I can give things to someone but often what I get back is

better. I remember when: _____

_____

_____

_____

The biggest miracle in my life was: _____

_____

_____

I like to top a gift with: _____

_____

_____

Cool Craft! Boot Gift Toppers

What You'll Need:

* 35 mm film canisters
* cardboard
* tissue paper
* ribbon
* scissors
* tape

What To Do:

1. Trace the foot pattern on the next page and cut it out.

2. Trace the pattern on cardboard and cut it out.

3. Crumple a small piece of tissue paper and tape it to the front of the shoe to stuff the toe.

4. Tape the film canister to the shoe heel.

5. Place the shoe on a large piece of tissue paper. Wrap the tissue paper around the shoe, bringing the ends over the tube. Tie the tissue paper around the film canister with ribbon.

6. Trim the tissue to about 1" higher than the film canister.

7. Fill the film canister with candy or Bible verses written on strips of paper.

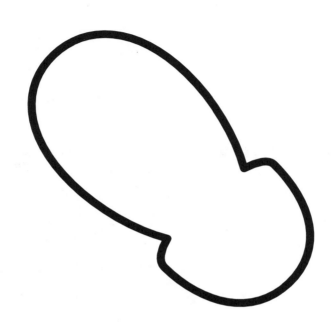

Sparkling Ideas

◎ Make these shoes as table favors for a missionary dinner. Add a slip of paper with the name of a missionary inside each one so that people can pray for the person in the shoe they receive!

◎ Make matching gift wrap with footprints. Write out Romans 10:15 on a slip of paper and place it in the shoe.

◎ Use the shoes as a reminder for your Sunday school class to follow Jesus. Stuff the shoes with candy because life is sweet with Him.

◎ Make a shoe as a gift topper for a friend who is moving. Add a slip of paper that says, "No matter where you travel, God will go with you." Add a prayer that your paths will cross again in the future.

◎ Make the shoes in pink or blue for baby shower favors. If you do not know of a baby shower, make them for a pregnancy crisis center and fill them with Scriptures about children, such as Matthew 18:2-5, 19:13-15 and Psalm 139:13-16.

◎ Make the shoes as nursing home favors and add notes asking the residents to share stories of where they traveled in life. Visit a nursing home and take time to listen to the experiences of the men and women who live there.

A Beautiful Believer
Enfolds Others with Love

Memory Verse

When this had dawned on him [Peter], he went to the house of Mary the mother of John, also called Mark, where many people had gathered and were praying.
– Acts 12:12

Mary, Mark's Mother

An angel rescued Peter from prison. As soon as Peter realized what had happened, he headed straight for the home of Mary, Mark's mother. He knew where he would be welcomed. Mary's home was a place where many people gathered to pray.

Little is known about Mary but much is known about her son. Her son wrote the gospel of Mark, accompanied Peter and helped Paul. Mary raised a faithful Christian son. Her home became a place of prayer, where many Christians felt welcomed and unafraid to express their faith through prayer.

In those days, welcoming Christians risked persecution. This trouble grew worse between Jews and Christians at Passover, a

Jewish holiday. Herod, to please the Jews, arrested Peter. But Mary stood firm in her faith. She was unafraid of welcoming Christians. Have you ever been afraid to let others know you are a Christian or to let someone see you pray? If so, pray and ask God to help you be strong.

God commands Christians to be hospitable and love one another. Make this gift wrap and remember to give others the gift of love.

Prayer

Lord, help me surround others with love. Let me feel brave to welcome my Christian friends and not hide my faith. Amen.

Dazzling Thoughts

◎ "Every good and perfect gift is from above, coming down from the Father of the heavenly lights, who does not change like shifting shadows." (James 1:17)

◎ Giving gifts reflects God's giving nature.

◎ When someone expresses joy at a gift, remind him or her of God's gift of eternal life that gives eternal joy.

◎ "He wraps up the waters in his clouds, yet the clouds do not burst under their weight." (Job 26:8) God uses clouds to wrap the gift of water, something people and the earth need. Make gift wrap with clouds on it.

◎ It takes time to wrap gifts. The time itself expresses love.

 # Journaling

Sometimes it's hard to express my hidden thoughts. The

hardest things for me to talk about are: _____

_____

_____

_____

_____

When I receive a gift wrapped with beautiful paper I feel: _____

_____

_____

_____

_____

People can't see God but they see His love through me. I'm like a

wrapping and I look like: _____

_____

_____

_____

_____

Cool Craft! Decorated Gift Wrap

What You'll Need:

* plain paper, brown or white
* craft foam
* paint
* colored ink stamp pad
* paper doilies
* sponge
* wood blocks or thread spools
* scissors

What To Do:

1. For lacy paper, place a lace doily on paper.

2. Dip a sponge in paint, lightly coating the sponge.

3. Sponge paint over the doily.

4. Remove the doily. This leaves a lacy design on the paper.

5. Repeat in several places.

6. For stamped paper, cut craft foam in a shape (some to try: heart, fish, cross).

7. Glue the foam cutout to an empty spool or block of wood.

8. Press the stamp on an ink pad.

9. Press the stamp onto paper.

10. Repeat all over the paper, at random, or to form a pattern.

Sparkling Ideas

◎ Cut snowflakes to use instead of doilies.

◎ Use decorated paper as the background in pictures you frame.

◎ Use decorated paper in photo and memory albums.

◎ Decorate a small piece of folded paper to match your paper and use it as a gift tag.

◎ Make paper that represents your favorite Scripture, such as hearts for a verse on love or crosses for a verse on forgiveness. Then write the verse on the wrapped package.

◎ If your church holds a bazaar, set up a gift wrap booth with the paper you make. Use the money you make to help others, or put it in your church's offering.

A Beautiful Believer Shares God's Word

Memory Verse

She said to her mistress, "If only my master would see the prophet who is in Samaria! He would cure him of his leprosy." – 2 Kings 5:3

Naaman's Servant Girl

A young girl spoke those words of faith. This unnamed girl wanted to help even though she had been captured and made a slave. She gave words of hope that led to a great healing. She felt badly seeing her master sick with leprosy.

The girl told her master's wife that her God could heal General Naaman. His wife listened, then passed along the message to Naaman. Naaman told the king of Arman what the girl said. The king also believed her.

The king of Arman wrote a letter asking the king of Israel to help. Naaman packed money and gifts to give as a reward for healing him. That showed great trust in the girl's words. Yet the king of Israel failed to trust God's power and expressed frustration at the letter. Elijah, the prophet, heard about the letter and told the king to send Naaman to him. He showed God's power by healing Naaman.

Decorate some paper for stationery, then use it to send messages expressing faith to others.

Prayer

Thank You, Father, for giving me Your written Word. Help me to be a messenger of the Gospel. Amen.

◎ Sending letters is a way of sending news or a message. Paul and other apostles wrote the letters in the Bible known as "the epistles."

◎ We are like letters, messages from God that are written on our hearts. Read about this in 2 Corinthians 3:1-3.

◎ It was common to take letters when visiting leaders in Bible times. Nehemiah took letters from the king with him when he went to rebuild Jerusalem. These important letters helped Nehemiah travel and receive supplies.

◎ The Bible is a set of love letters from God, our king.

 Journaling

The last time I wrote a letter was: _____

_____

The most important news I can write in a letter is: _____

_____

_____

_____

_____

The last time I received a letter was: _____

_____

My favorite Scripture, or love letter from God, is: _____

_____

_____

_____

_____

Cool Craft! Decorated Stationery

What You'll Need:

* white paper
* craft foam
* small wood blocks or foam core scraps
* glue
* ink pads in assorted colors
* scissors

What To Do:

1. Cut a tiny shape from the craft foam.

2. Glue the shape to a wood block or to foam core. You can cut separate shapes to make a mini scene, such as a fish and waves.

3. Press the stamp shape onto an ink pad.

4. Lay paper flat or fold it to form a card. Decorate the paper with the stamps.

Sparkling Ideas

◎ Stamp the envelope flap, too.

◎ Try using a rainbow stamp pad for a colorful stamp.

◎ If you make an animal stamp, punch out the eyes with a hole punch.

◎ Use the stamps to decorate plain paper book covers for school books.

◎ Make your own memo sheets. Cut paper into note-sized pieces and stamp the corners.

◎ Make stamps as gifts and give the recipient plain stationery as part of the gift.

◎ Fold paper in fourths. Cut out a window opening on the top fold. Slide a colored piece of paper between the top layers and glue it in place. Stamp around the opening.

◎ Fold ⅓ inward from each end of a sheet of paper to make a card that opens like double doors.

A Beautiful Believer Responds to People in Need

Memory Verse

So they called Rebekah and asked her, "Will you go with this man?" "I will go," she said.
– Genesis 24:58

Rebekah

Rebekah's response to a servant's request changed her life. He asked for a drink. She gave him a drink and also offered to water his camels. She drew water from the well until the camels were satisfied.

Abraham sent his most trusted servant to find a wife for Isaac. The servant prayed for God to reveal His choice of a bride. As a sign, the servant prayed that the right woman would offer water to his camels. God answered the prayer through Rebekah.

The servant explained to Rebekah's family how God chose her as Isaac's bride. Her family agreed but wanted time with her before she left. Rebekah showed her willingness to serve God when the servant asked to go immediately and Rebekah responded, "I will go." Her generous nature and willingness to accept God's will showed a giving heart.

Do you have a willing heart? Do you ever offer to do more than you are asked? Make these hearts to give. Write on the hearts what you will do to show love.

Prayer

Lord, help me be a willing servant. Teach me to respond to the needs of others. Amen.

Dazzling Thoughts

◎ Giving from a loving heart is the greatest way to express God's love. Jesus said, "By this all men will know that you are my disciples, if you love one another." (John 13:35)

◎ The heart cut-out opens to a cross as a reminder that Jesus died on the cross, making Himself a bridge to heaven.

◎ When we love someone we are willing to put them first and make sacrifices.

◎ If we fill our hearts with Christian love we will respond to the needs of others with love.

◎ Folded paper cut into a heart and then opened multiplies the number of hearts cut. When we give love we receive more love in return.

◎ "Let us not become weary in doing good, for at the proper time we will reap a harvest if we do not give up." (Galatians 6:9)

◎ Read Galatians 6:7-8 to discover what you can reap.

Journaling

Sometimes I have to choose whether to have fun or to do something for someone in need. One time that I chose to help someone else was: _____

_____

_____

_____

_____

It's good to give a valentine any time because: _____

_____

_____

_____

_____

The people in my life who sacrifice for me are: _____

_____

_____

Cool Craft! Paper Hearts

What You'll Need:

* pink paper
* scissors

What To Do:

1. Measure and cut your pink paper until it is an 8" square.

2. Fold the paper in half diagonally.

3. Open the paper. Fold it diagonally again, using the opposite corners. Open.

4. Turn the paper over. Fold the paper in half from side-to-side. Open.

5. Turn the paper over. Fold the last fold inward, matching the folds while folding along the first two diagonally folded lines. This is called a "valley fold." Fold the paper flat into a triangle.

6. Use the heart pattern on the next page to cut out a heart. Place the pattern on the triangle with the fold at the bottom. Be careful not to cut the fold apart. When you open the paper, you will see a cross in the center.

7. Trace the other pattern on another folded square, again being careful to not cut the folds. When you open the paper, you will see four girls joined together with hearts. A cross will be in the center.

Sparkling Ideas

- ◎ Fold the paper and make your own designs to cut.
- ◎ Try not cutting in the center cross. Punch a hole near the center while the paper is folded and add an elastic thread to make a wrist band. Use it as an address booklet for friends to fill in names and phone numbers.
- ◎ Make hearts as invitations to invite people to church.
- ◎ Cut Christmas trees with a cross in the center when opened. Glue white paper over the open cross. Write "He came for all" on the cross so that the words cross at the As. Then add, "Join God's family tree. Merry Christmas."

154

A Beautiful Believer Chooses Wisely

Memory Verse

"Martha, Martha," the Lord answered, "you are worried and upset about many things." – Luke 10:41

Martha

How exciting to have Jesus come for a visit! Martha bustled around the kitchen, preparing a meal for Jesus. She knew how He fed 5,000 with only a few loaves of bread and two fish, yet she worried about this meal. Martha complained to Jesus and asked Him to tell her sister, Mary, to help her.

How did Jesus respond? He didn't do what Martha asked. He told Martha that she was too worried about unimportant things. He went on to tell Martha that Mary made the wiser choice. Mary chose to sit and listen to Jesus. Jesus was a guest in the house and Mary took time to be with her guest.

Jesus showed concern for Martha. He repeated her name to get her attention and help slow her down. He pointed out a wiser decision. Sometimes Jesus does not answer our prayers the way we want because He knows the best answer to give us.

Make and shape this bunny bread. Be sure to make it ahead of time so you have time to spend with guests. Let them know some "bunny loves" them!

Prayer

Jesus, help me to use my time wisely. When I pray and read the Bible, help me put aside other thoughts and spend the time focused on You. Amen.

Dazzling Thoughts

◎ Prepare for guests before their arrival. Plan a time to share food and talk about Jesus. Put out the plates, glasses and napkins ahead of time. Have the drinks ready to pour. Then spend the time visiting with your friends.

◎ The following recipe is for bunny bread. One reason a rabbit is used as a symbol of Easter is because a rabbit hops up from an empty hole in the ground, like Jesus rose from the dead.

◎ Bread rises in a warm oven. With warmth in our speech we can reach out to help people change.

◎ The dough is soft and easy to shape before it is cooked. We need to be gentle and willing to let God shape our lives.

◎ Warm bread smells good. The Bible says Christians are fragrant. Read this in 2 Corinthians 2:14-16.

 Journaling

God has been shaping my life. He: _____

_____

_____

_____

_____

It takes time to make bread. It takes time for God to help me

change and grow. I'm changing right now. I'm becoming: ____

_____

_____

_____

_____

Jesus shared bread with His disciples. I can share bread with:

_____

_____

Cool Craft! Some-Bunny Bread

What You'll Need:

* bread dough (store-bought or use recipe on next page)
* pretzel sticks
* melted butter
* baking sheet
* hot pads

What To Do:

1. Preheat the oven to 400 degrees.
2. Unroll the dough.

OUCH!

3. Pull off pieces of dough and shape it into balls: one 3" ball, one 2" ball and two 1" balls.
4. Use the large ball to shape the body.
5. Use the medium ball to shape the head and press it onto the body.
6. Shape the small balls into ears and press them onto the head.
7. With small pieces of dough, form a nose and eyes (or use raisins). Add rabbit paws if desired, formed from dough. Add the cotton tail.
8. Stick in thin pretzel sticks for whiskers.
9. Brush the bread lightly with melted butter. Bake 20 minutes or until lightly browned. Use hot pads to carefully remove the bread from the oven.

OUCH!

Bread Recipe

- 1 cup warm water
- 4 teaspoons cooking oil
- 2¾ cups unbleached flour
- 1 teaspoon salt
- 2 teaspoons sugar
- 1¼ teaspoons dry yeast

Mix the dry ingredients together. Mix the water and oil in a bowl. Add the dry ingredients. Mix well. Place the dough on a floured surface. Knead it for five minutes. Place it in a greased bowl. Cover and let the dough rise until it doubles (1-2 hours). Punch down the dough. Turn it onto floured surface. Shape. Let the dough rise 15 minutes more.

Sparkling Ideas

- Make bunny bread to give. Add a note that says, "Some bunny loves you."
- Make other bread shapes, such as hearts, trees, wreaths or fish.
- Invite friends for an "agape" meal. Break bread together and share thoughts about Jesus.
- Make bread for neighbors.
- Make bread for the homeless and add a note: "God made every bunny special– you're some bunny special, too."
- Make bunny bread for Easter and share it with your family.
- Look up recipes for bread dough art and make a small bunny bread as a decoration. Tie a ribbon around the bunny's neck.

A Beautiful Believer
Sticks Close to Jesus

Memory Verse

Joanna the wife of Cuza, the manager of Herod's household; Susanna; and many others. These women were helping to support them out of their own means.
– Luke 8:3

Joanna

How do you spend your money? Joanna, Susanna and other Bible women used their own money to support Jesus and His disciples. These women had something else in common: Jesus had healed them all. Jesus cured them of evil spirits and diseases. With thankful hearts, these women followed Jesus and supported Him.

Who was Joanna?

Joanna's husband held a high position, working for Herod. Herod was a Roman official who ruled the Jewish people. He lived an evil life and made many wicked decisions. He even had John the Baptist put to death. Joanna cared more about serving Jesus than her husband's position. She chose to follow Jesus instead of enjoying a wealthy life at Herod's palace.

Joanna and other women gave generously rather than buy fancy clothes and jewelry. Think about which things are most important to you. How important is Jesus to you? How close do you want to be to Him? Make this refrigerator magnet as a reminder to stick close to Jesus.

Prayer

Thank You, Lord, for the blessings You give me. Help me to follow You and support church leaders. Amen.

Dazzling Thoughts

◎ Peas grow together in a pod, sharing the same protection, water and food.

◎ Just as the peas stay together through wind and storms, God stays with you always. (Matthew 28:20).

◎ A magnet is attracted to the opposite pole. We are often attracted to sin but must learn to cling to God.

◎ Christians need to be with other Christians. Read some reasons why in Hebrews 10:24-25.

 # Journaling

It's hard to stay close to Jesus when: _____

_____

_____

_____

I'm happy that Jesus is always with me because: _____

_____

_____

_____

Like peas in a pod my Christian friend _____

and I do things together. We: _____

_____

_____

_____

Going to church helps me: _____

_____

_____

_____

I will help You, Jesus, by: _____

_____

_____

Cool Craft! Peas in a Pod Magnets

What You'll Need:

* ❋ white paper
* ❋ two 1½" green pom-poms
* ❋ four wiggle eyes
* ❋ craft glue
* ❋ green felt square
* ❋ magnet strip
* ❋ scissors

What To Do:

1. Trace the pod pattern on the next page on white paper and cut it out.

2. Trace the pattern on green felt and cut it out.

3. Glue the eyes onto the pom-poms.

4. Glue the pom-poms together in the center of the pod.

5. Glue the pod's ends together and to the pom-poms.

6. Glue a magnet strip on the back of the felt.

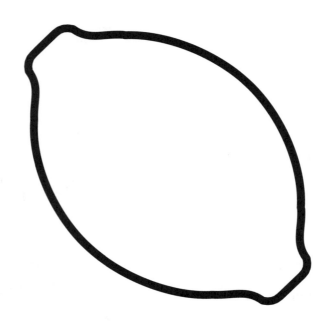

✳ ✳ ✳ ✳ ✳ ✳ ✳ ✳
✳ Sparkling Ideas ✳
✳ ✳ ✳ ✳ ✳ ✳ ✳ ✳ ✳

◎ Use craft foam to cut out and make other types of refrigerator magnets.

◎ With colored pom-poms and a strip of black felt, make a caterpillar magnet. Add a note that God transforms people from the inside out.

◎ Make Peas in a Pod Magnets as gift toppers or party favors.

◎ Use a pin back instead of a magnet on your Peas in a Pod and wear it!

◎ Make Peas in a Pod as a symbol of friendship for a friend.

◎ Make Peas in a Pod as an anniversary gift for a couple you admire.

A Beautiful Believer Serves Others

Memory Verse

He touched her hand and the fever left her, and she got up and began to wait on him. – Matthew 8:15

Peter's Mother-in-law

A healing touch brought Peter's mother-in-law to her feet. She lived in Peter's home, so she was probably a widow with no sons of her own to support her. Jesus entered the house and saw her lying sick in bed. In response to seeing her pain, Jesus reached out to heal her. A fever was not too small for Jesus to care about and heal. No one even asked Jesus to help.

Think of times Jesus showed His love even though you didn't ask Him.

This woman, like so many others in the Bible, remains unnamed. Her name is not important. The story allows us to see Jesus and how people responded to Him. Her example of caring for Jesus as soon as she received healing gives us an example of Christian behavior. She looked and found ways to wait on Him.

When Jesus reaches out to us and blesses us, we should

respond by finding ways to serve Him. Serve Jesus by making these finger puppets and using them to tell children about Him.

Prayer

Lord, thank You for loving me. Help me to serve others. Amen.

Dazzling Thoughts

◎ Jesus used his finger to change a bad situation into a good lesson. A group of people were angry with a woman. As Jesus wrote on the ground, He said that any of the angry people who had not sinned could throw a stone at the woman. Of course, there was no one who had not sinned, so the group went away and left the woman alone. Jesus made them understand they were no better than the woman. (John 8:3-11)

◎ We can point out other's faults with our fingers or use our fingers to give a message of love. The choice is up to each person.

◎ We use our fingers to touch. Jesus' touch healed people. Check it out in Matthew 9:18-22.

◎ Angels are messengers. Look up these Scriptures: Matthew 24:31, Luke 15:10; Psalm 34:7; and Matthew 18:10.

 # Journaling

I can be a secret angel for someone today. I can:

_____

_____

_____

Grace is an undeserved favor from God. I'm thankful for God's

grace because: _____

_____

_____

_____

I can use my fingers to: _____

_____

_____

_____

When I'm healthy, I can serve others by: _____

_____

_____

_____

Cool Craft! Angel Puppet Favors

What You'll Need:

* ✳ 3" paper doilies
* ✳ pink paper
* ✳ scrap paper
* ✳ scissors
* ✳ pink pencil
* ✳ glue

What To Do:

1. Trace and cut out the pattern on the next page.

2. Place the pattern on the doily and cut out the angel.

3. Cut slits on the angel as indicated by the dashed lines.

4. Slide the slits together to form a puppet that stands up.

5. You may leave the angel's arms apart as shown, or fold them inward and glue a pink paper heart between the hands.

6. Or, buy paper drinking cones, fill them with candy and tape plastic wrap over the top. Turn it upside-down and place the angel on top of the cone.

✳ Sparkling Ideas

◎ Make finger puppets from craft foam for more permanent angels.

◎ Use foil paper for shimmering angels.

◎ Add glitter to the angel's halo and bottom edge with a glitter pen or glue and glitter.

◎ Use a needle and thread and attach a string to change the angel into an ornament.

◎ Use as gift toppers.

A Beautiful Believer Receives Eternal Life

Memory Verse

"Don't be alarmed," he said. " You are looking for Jesus the Nazarene, who was crucified. He has risen! He is not here. See the place where they laid him." – Mark 16:6

Salome

Who is talking and who is listening in this verse? An angel spoke to Salome and two other women at the empty tomb. Jesus had risen! These women, who arrived at dawn, heard the news first.

Salome, the mother of James and John, stood at the foot of the cross. Now she stood at the empty tomb. She saw the two most important events in Jesus' life. How did she react? She fled, trembling and bewildered. The women kept silent although the angel told them to tell others the Good News. Later, Mary Magdalene told the disciples the news, but there's no word about what Salome did.

Many people understand that Jesus died and recognize that believing in Him and His resurrection gives them eternal life. Yet many of the same people react with fear and never share the Good News.

Do you tell others about Jesus? If not, start now. Make and wear an empty tomb necklace to remember to share the Good News and what the empty tomb means.

Prayer

Lord, help me tell others about You. Help me bring words of life to empty hearts. Amen.

Dazzling Thoughts

◎ The empty tomb showed Jesus had risen. Use the necklace as a way to tell others about Jesus.

◎ The necklace is shaped from clay. A potter shapes clay. God calls Himself a potter and says we are the clay. (Jeremiah 18:1-6)

◎ Pharaoh rewarded Joseph and put a gold necklace around his neck (Genesis 41:42). Let your necklace remind you of the reward of eternal life.

Journaling

When I think of the empty tomb I think about: _____

_____

_____

_____

The clay takes the form I give it. I want to let God shape me

because: _____

_____

_____

I hope the shape God chooses for me is: _____

_____

_____

I told: _____

about Jesus when: _____

_____

_____

One person I want to talk to about Jesus is: _____

_____

 **Cool Craft!**

Empty Tomb Clay Necklace

What You'll Need:

* clay that bakes in an oven
* cord
* baking sheet
* scissors
* knife or craft stick
* pen

What To Do:

1. Shape the clay in one of two ways:

Clay Shape 1

1. Shape the clay into a 1" ball.
2. Flatten the bottom of the ball. Carve out a hole in the center of the ball all the way through the clay, using a knife or craft stick.
3. Prick a design on the back of the tomb, such as your initials or a butterfly.

Clay Shape 2

1. Form a long tube and shape the clay according to the pattern at right.
2. Prick a design on the back.

2. Bake according to the package directions. OUCH!

3. Cut a cord to use as a necklace. Fold it in half. Put the fold

173

through the hole to make a larkshead knot (see page 90).

4. Tie the ends together to form a necklace.

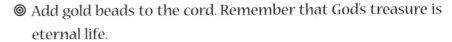

Sparkling Ideas

◎ Add gold beads to the cord. Remember that God's treasure is eternal life.

◎ Glue on a tiny butterfly as a reminder of new life.

◎ Make these for a mother-daughter celebration as reminders that women were the first to see Jesus.

◎ Make a necklace as a gift to someone for her or his baptism.

◎ Make and send one to a friend, with an invitation to accept Jesus.

◎ Visit a young Sunday school class, show the necklace, give your testimony and then invite the children to make necklaces. (You can have them make paper ones if you don't have enough clay.)

* Shopping List *

In addition to the basic tools listed on pages 13-16, you will need some or all of the following items to complete the crafts in *God's Girls!* Look for these items in craft stores, discount stores or even in your own house! Check off the items as you gather them.

❏ acrylic paint or spray paint

❏ aluminum foil

❏ artificial flowers

❏ baking sheet

❏ basket with handle

❏ beads

❏ bread dough (or use recipe and ingredients on page 159)

❏ butter, melted

❏ can, tuna or cat food

❏ candle, long taper

❏ canvas bag

❏ cardboard, plain and white

❏ cartons, pint-size milk or juice

❏ cellophane, colored

❏ chenille stems

❏ clay or florist's foam block

❏ clay, baking

❏ construction paper

❏ cord

❏ cotton fabric scraps

❏ craft cord

❏ craft foam

❏ crepe paper streamers

❏ cutting board or waxed paper

❏ earring backings

❏ fabric markers, black and green

❏ fabric paint, green and three other colors

❏ felt, green

❏ film canisters, 35mm size

❏ florist wire

❏ gift wrap

❏ hair bands, barrettes or pony tail bands

❏ hair comb, plastic

❏ hot pads

❏ jingle bells

❏ lace scraps

❏ magazines, used

❏ magnet strip

❏ markers, permanent and non-permanent

❏ masking tape, 1" wide

❏ measuring tape

- ❏ metallic cord or macramé cord
- ❏ needlepoint needle
- ❏ needlepoint yarn or metallic cord
- ❏ paint, white and red
- ❏ paint brushes
- ❏ paint roller or wooden dowel
- ❏ paper: white, brown, gray, pink
- ❏ paper doilies
- ❏ paper plate
- ❏ pen
- ❏ pencil, pink
- ❏ pin backs
- ❏ plastic cup
- ❏ plastic fruit
- ❏ plastic needlepoint canvas
- ❏ plastic photo block
- ❏ pom-poms, ½" size green and other colors
- ❏ poster board, heavy
- ❏ pretzel sticks
- ❏ quilter's tape, ¼" wide
- ❏ ribbon
- ❏ sandpaper
- ❏ sequins
- ❏ shoe box
- ❏ silk leaves or real leaves
- ❏ soda bottle, plastic
- ❏ sponge
- ❏ stamp pad, colored ink
- ❏ star stickers
- ❏ straight pin
- ❏ T-shirt, plain white
- ❏ tape
- ❏ tennis shoes, plain with laces
- ❏ thread, white
- ❏ tiny toys, stickers or coins
- ❏ tissue paper
- ❏ toilet paper roll
- ❏ toothpick
- ❏ wiggle eyes, 10 mm size
- ❏ wooden blocks
- ❏ wood cutouts, assorted star shapes
- ❏ wooden doll head or plain bead
- ❏ wooden hearts, 1" size
- ❏ wooden manicure stick or chopstick
- ❏ yarn: white and other colors

✳ ✳ ✳ ✳ ✳ ✳ ✳ ✳ ✳

* Memory Verses *

How's your memory? See how well you can remember these Scriptures from *God's Girls!* Need help? Look up the page numbers and try again!

Genesis 16:13 65

Genesis 21:6................44

Genesis 24:58 150

Genesis 3:20................73

Exodus 2:3 129

Exodus 15:20...............18

Joshua 6:25 87

Judges 5:31 107

Ruth 3:11 28

1 Samuel 1:10 38

1 Kings 17:24 134

2 Kings 5:3 145

Esther 2:17..................83

Psalm 68:25 54

Matthew 8:15 165

Mark 16:6 170

Luke 1:38.......................78

Luke 1:45.......................23

Luke 2:38 33

Luke 8:3 160

Luke 10:41.....................155

Luke 21:3-4...................97

John 4:14 49

Acts 12:12 140

Acts 16:14 102

Acts 17:24......................112

Acts 18:26......................92

Romans 16:2 124

Romans 16:12 117

Colossians 3:12............59

If You Liked *God's Girls!* You'll Love *God and Me!*

God and Me! is a series of devotionals for girls. Each age-level book is packed with over 100 devotionals, plus memory verses, stories, journal space and fun activities to help you learn more about the Bible. Visit your favorite Christian bookstore to find *God and Me!* and other Legacy Press books created just for you.

LP46821
ISBN 1-885358-61-X

LP46822
ISBN 1-885358-60-1

LP46823
ISBN 1-885358-54-7

Available in the New International Version (NIV) and the King James version (KJV) of the Bible.

Get Cooking in the Word with *Gobble Up the Bible*!

For ages 5-12, this cookbook will help you learn to make really great food and grow closer to God as you do it. Each of the more than 70 recipes includes a fun activity. Includes a bonus section on kitchen safety and basic cooking techniques. **FREE** set of measuring spoons attached to each book!

LP46811
ISBN 1-885358-59-8

Journals Just for You!

My Bible Journal is one of a series of journals you will love! The daily devotionals will make you want to dig into your Bible, the stories will make you think and the journal space will help you praise and pray to God.

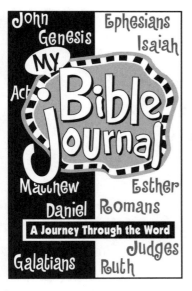

Get the whole set!

My Bible Journal	ISBN 1-885358-70-9	LP46911
My Bible Journal (KJV Edition)	ISBN 1-885358-86-5	LP46912
My Answer Journal	ISBN 1-885358-72-5	LP46931
My Praise Journal	ISBN 1-885358-71-7	LP46921
My Prayer Journal	ISBN 1-885358-37-7	DB46731
My Wisdom Journal	ISBN 1-885358-73-3	LP46941

Visit your favorite Christian bookstore to find other Legacy Press books created just for you.